Math in Focus®

Singapore Math
by Marshall Cavendish

Workbook

Consultant and Author
Dr. Fong Ho Kheong

Authors
Gan Kee Soon and Chelvi Ramakrishnan

U.S. Consultants
Dr. Richard Bisk, Andy Clark, and Patsy F. Kanter

Marshall Cavendish
Education

U.S. Distributor

Houghton
Mifflin
Harcourt

COMMON
CORE

© Copyright 2009, 2013 Edition Marshall Cavendish International (Singapore) Private Limited

Published by Marshall Cavendish Education
An imprint of Marshall Cavendish International (Singapore) Private Limited
Times Centre, 1 New Industrial Road, Singapore 536196
Customer Service Hotline: (65) 6213 9444
E-mail: tmesales@sg.marshallcavendish.com
Website: www.marshallcavendish.com/education

Distributed by
Houghton Mifflin Harcourt
222 Berkeley Street
Boston, MA 02116
Tel: 617-351-5000
Website: www.hmheducation.com/mathinfocus

First published 2009
2013 Edition

Math in Focus® Grade 5 Workbook B
ISBN 978-0-669-01338-2

Printed in Singapore

8 9 10   1401   18 17 16 15 14
4500457654   A B C D E

Contents

Decimals

Multiplying and Dividing Decimals

10 Percent

11 Graphs and Probability

12 Angles

13 Properties of Triangles and Four-sided Figures

14 Three-Dimensional Shapes

15 Surface Area and Volume

Decimals

Practice 1   Understanding Thousandths

Write the decimal shown in each place-value chart.

Example

Ones	Tenths	Hundredths	Thousandths
	○ ○	○ ○ ○	○ ○ ○ ○ ○ ○ ○

_0.237_

1.

Ones	Tenths	Hundredths	Thousandths
○ ○ ○ ○		○ ○ ○ ○ ○	○ ○ ○ ○ ○

_____

2.

Ones	Tenths	Hundredths	Thousandths
○ ○ ○ ○ ○ ○			○ ○ ○ ○ ○ ○ ○ ○ ○

_____

Write the decimal shown in the place-value chart.

3.

Ones	Tenths	Hundredths	Thousandths
○ ○ ○ ○ ○	○ ○	○	

_____

Mark X to show where each decimal is located.

4.   0.006   **5.**   0.024   **6.**   0.033

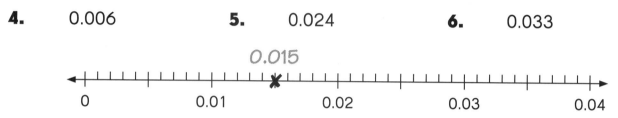

0.015

0   0.01   0.02   0.03   0.04

Write the decimal shown by each arrow.

7.

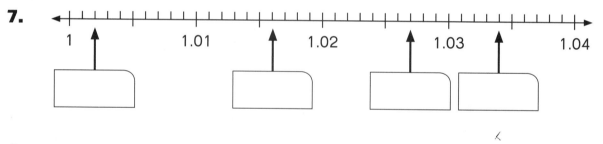

1   1.01   1.02   1.03   1.04

Complete.

8.   4 hundredths = _____ thousandths

9.   8 tenths 5 hundredths = _____ thousandths

10.   20 thousandths = _____ hundredths

11.   125 thousandths = 1 tenth _____ thousandths

Practice 2 Comparing and Rounding Decimals

Compare the decimals in each place-value chart.

Fill in the blanks. Write > or < in the ( ).

> **Example**
>
> | Ones | Tenths | Hundredths | Thousandths |
> |:---:|:---:|:---:|:---:|
> | 0 | 0 | 2 | |
> | 0 | 0 | 1 | 5 |
>
> _0.02_ is greater than _0.015_ .
>
> _0.02_ (>) _0.015_

1.

Ones	Tenths	Hundredths	Thousandths
0	3	0	8
0	2	9	

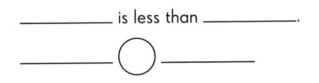

_____ is less than _____ .

_____ ( ) _____

2.

Ones	Tenths	Hundredths	Thousandths
4	0	9	1
4	1	9	

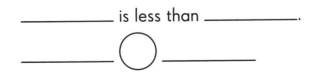

_____ is less than _____ .

_____ ( ) _____

Write the greater decimal.

3.   11.6 or 21.8 _____

4.   10.55 or 10.05 _____

5.   20.07 or 20.01 _____

6.   100.202 or 100.212 _____

Write >, <, or = in each ◯.

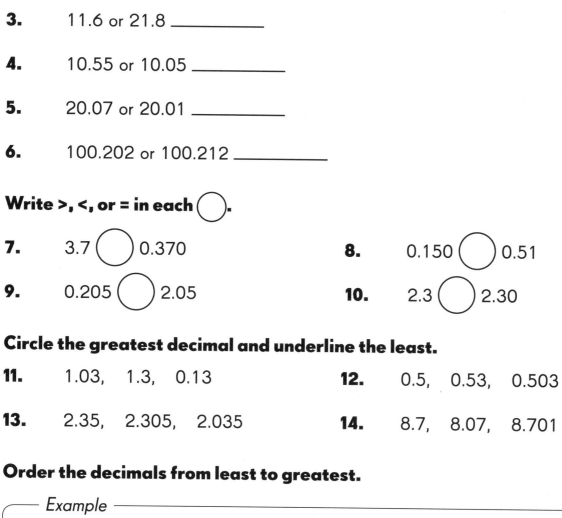

7.   3.7 ◯ 0.370   **8.**   0.150 ◯ 0.51

9.   0.205 ◯ 2.05   **10.**   2.3 ◯ 2.30

Circle the greatest decimal and underline the least.

11.   1.03,   1.3,   0.13   **12.**   0.5,   0.53,   0.503

13.   2.35,   2.305,   2.035   **14.**   8.7,   8.07,   8.701

Order the decimals from least to greatest.

> *Example*
>
> 3.33,   3.03,   3.303   3.03,   3.303,   3.33

15.   5.51,   5.051,   5.501   _____

16.   4,   4.01,   4.001   _____

17.   0.023,   0.203,   0.230   _____

Write the missing decimal in each box. Round the given decimal to the nearest hundredth.

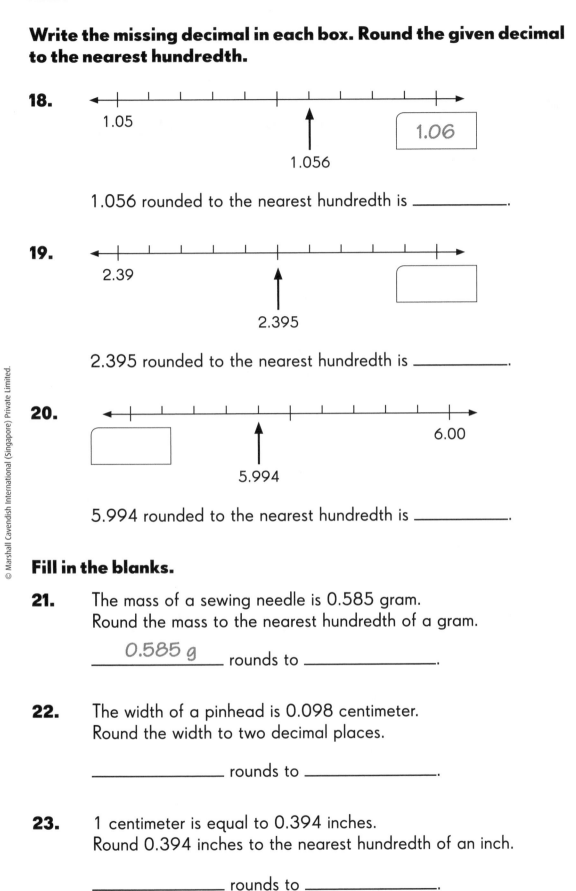

18.

1.05

1.06

1.056

1.056 rounded to the nearest hundredth is _____.

19.

2.39

2.395

2.395 rounded to the nearest hundredth is _____.

20.

6.00

5.994

5.994 rounded to the nearest hundredth is _____.

Fill in the blanks.

21. The mass of a sewing needle is 0.585 gram.
Round the mass to the nearest hundredth of a gram.

_____0.585 g_____ rounds to _____.

22. The width of a pinhead is 0.098 centimeter.
Round the width to two decimal places.

_____ rounds to _____.

23. 1 centimeter is equal to 0.394 inches.
Round 0.394 inches to the nearest hundredth of an inch.

_____ rounds to _____.

Round each decimal to the nearest whole number, nearest tenth, and nearest hundredth.

24.

Decimal	Rounded to the Nearest		
	Whole Number	Tenth	Hundredth
1.049			
3.753			
2.199			

Fill in the blanks.

25. A decimal rounded to the nearest tenth is 2.5.
Write two decimals that can be rounded to 2.5.

_____ and _____

26. A decimal rounded to the nearest hundredth is 4.09.
Write two decimals that can be rounded to 4.09.

_____ and _____

27. A decimal rounded to the nearest hundredth is 6.32.
This decimal is greater than 6.32.

What could this decimal be? _____

28. A decimal rounded to the nearest hundredth is 7.01.
This decimal is less than 7.01.

What could this decimal be? _____

Practice 3 Rewriting Decimals as Fractions and Mixed Numbers

Rewrite each decimal as a fraction or mixed number in simplest form.

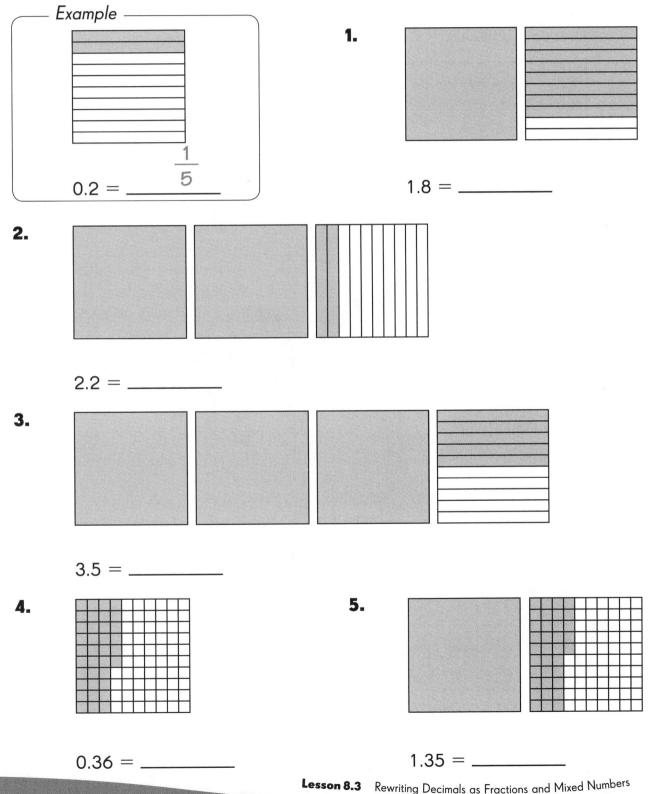

Example

$0.2 = \dfrac{1}{5}$

1.

$1.8 = $ _____

2.

$2.2 = $ _____

3.

$3.5 = $ _____

4.

$0.36 = $ _____

5.

$1.35 = $ _____

Rewrite each decimal as a fraction or mixed number in simplest form.

6.

1.12 = _____

7.

3.57 = _____

8.

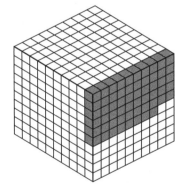

0.058 = _____

9.

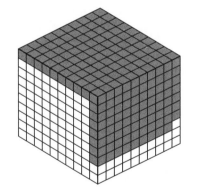

0.169 = _____

10.

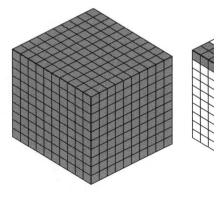

1.092 = _____

Rewrite the decimal as a mixed number in simplest form.

11.

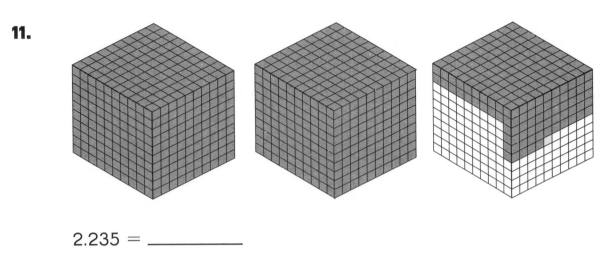

2.235 = _____

Rewrite each decimal as a fraction or mixed number in simplest form.

12. 7.3

13. 26.9

14. 0.59

15. 15.82

16. 1.28

17. 4.109

18. 0.136

19. 3.602

Math Journal

1. Explain why 1.8, 1.80, and 1.800 have the same value.

2. Howard does not know how to find the values of A and B on the number line. Write the steps Howard should use to find these values.

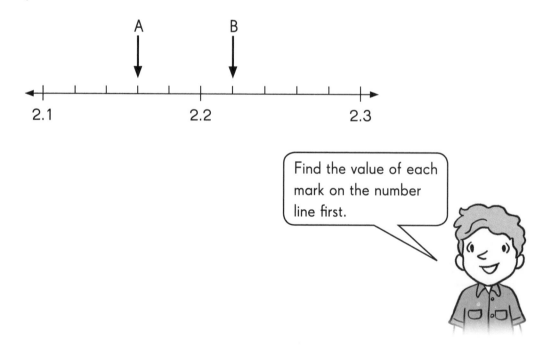

Find the value of each mark on the number line first.

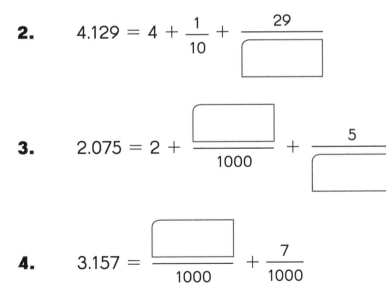

Put On Your Thinking Cap!

Challenging Practice

Solve.

1. You are given two numbers, 3.987 and 70.140.

    a. Round each number to the nearest tenth.

    b. Round each number to the nearest hundredth.

    c. Find the difference between your rounded answers for 3.987.

    d Find the difference between your rounded answers for 70.140.

    e. Are your answers in Exercises **a** and **b** the same? Explain why or why not.

Complete.

2. $4.129 = 4 + \dfrac{1}{10} + \dfrac{29}{\boxed{}}$

3. $2.075 = 2 + \dfrac{\boxed{}}{1000} + \dfrac{5}{\boxed{}}$

4. $3.157 = \dfrac{\boxed{}}{1000} + \dfrac{7}{1000}$

Put On Your Thinking Cap!

Problem Solving

Solve. Show your work.

1. Kimberly has 3.25 kilograms of flour in a container. She adds 45 grams of flour to the container. How many kilograms of flour does she have now?

2. The weight of four objects are $3\frac{1}{5}$ pounds, $3\frac{39}{1000}$ pounds, $3\frac{99}{100}$ pounds and $3\frac{52}{10}$ pounds. Arrange the weights in order from least to greatest.

Multiplying and Dividing Decimals

Practice 1   Multiplying Decimals

Multiply. Write the product as a decimal.

> *Example*
>
> $2 \times 0.3 = 2 \times \underline{\quad 3 \quad}$ tenths
>
> $ = \underline{\quad 6 \quad}$ tenths
>
> $ = \underline{\quad 0.6 \quad}$
>
> So, $2 \times 0.3 = \underline{\quad 0.6 \quad}$.

1. $5 \times 0.6 = 5 \times \underline{\qquad}$ tenths

$ = \underline{\qquad}$ tenths

$ = \underline{\qquad}$ or $\underline{\qquad}$

So, $5 \times 0.6 = \underline{\qquad}$.

2. $7 \times 0.8 = 7 \times \underline{\qquad}$ tenths

$ = \underline{\qquad}$ tenths

$ = \underline{\qquad}$

So, $7 \times 0.8 = \underline{\qquad}$.

3. $10 \times 0.4 = 10 \times \underline{\qquad}$ tenths

$ = \underline{\qquad}$ tenths

$ = \underline{\qquad}$ or $\underline{\qquad}$

So, $10 \times 0.4 = \underline{\qquad}$.

Multiply. Write the product as a decimal.

Example

$$3 \times 0.03 = 3 \times \underline{\quad 3 \quad} \text{ hundredths}$$

$$= \underline{\quad 9 \quad} \text{ hundredths}$$

$$= \underline{\quad 0.09 \quad}$$

So, $3 \times 0.03 = \underline{\quad 0.09 \quad}$.

4. $5 \times 0.02 = 5 \times \underline{\hspace{2cm}} \text{ hundredths}$

$$= \underline{\hspace{2cm}} \text{ hundredths}$$

$$= \underline{\hspace{1.5cm}} \text{ or } \underline{\hspace{1.5cm}}$$

So, $5 \times 0.02 = \underline{\hspace{1.5cm}}$.

5. $7 \times 0.07 = 7 \times \underline{\hspace{1.5cm}} \text{ hundredths}$

$$= \underline{\hspace{1.5cm}} \text{ hundredths}$$

$$= \underline{\hspace{1.5cm}}$$

So, $7 \times 0.07 = \underline{\hspace{1.5cm}}$.

6. $6 \times 0.12 = 6 \times \underline{\hspace{1.5cm}} \text{ hundredths}$

$$= \underline{\hspace{1.5cm}} \text{ hundredths}$$

$$= \underline{\hspace{1.5cm}}$$

So, $6 \times 0.12 = \underline{\hspace{1.5cm}}$.

Follow the steps to multiply 2.6 by 3. Fill in the blanks.

7.   Step 1

$\begin{array}{r} 2.6 \\ \times\quad 3 \\ \hline \end{array}$

Multiply the tenths by 3.

3×6 tenths = _____ tenths

Regroup the tenths.

_____ tenths = _____ one and _____ tenths

Step 2

$\begin{array}{r} 2.6 \\ \times\quad 3 \\ \hline \end{array}$

Multiply the ones by 3.

3×2 ones = _____ ones

Add the ones.

_____ ones + _____ one = _____ ones

So, $3 \times 2.6 =$ _____.

Multiply.

8. $\begin{array}{r} 0.3 \\ \times\quad 8 \\ \hline \end{array}$

9. $\begin{array}{r} 2.6 \\ \times\quad 4 \\ \hline \end{array}$

10. $\begin{array}{r} 7.9 \\ \times\quad 5 \\ \hline \end{array}$

11. $\begin{array}{r} 12.4 \\ \times\quad 7 \\ \hline \end{array}$

Follow the steps to multiply 1.46 by 6. Fill in the blanks.

12.

$$\begin{array}{r} 1.46 \\ \times 6 \\ \hline \end{array}$$

Multiply the hundredths by 6.

6 × 6 hundredths = _____ hundredths

Regroup the hundredths.

_____ hundredths = _____ tenths _____ hundredths

Step 2

$$\begin{array}{r} 1.46 \\ \times 6 \\ \hline \end{array}$$

Multiply the tenths by 6.

6 × 4 tenths = _____ tenths

Add the tenths.

_____ tenths + _____ tenths = _____ tenths

Regroup the tenths.

_____ tenths = _____ ones and _____ tenths

Step 3

$$\begin{array}{r} 1.46 \\ \times 6 \\ \hline \end{array}$$

Multiply the ones by 6.

6 × 1 one = _____ ones

Add the ones.

_____ ones + _____ ones = _____ ones

So, 6 × 1.46 = _____.

Multiply.

24. 1.3 × 100 = _____

25. 6.8 × 100 = _____

26. 4.196 × 100 = _____

27. 100 × 74.3 = _____

28. 46.8 × 100 = _____

29. 4.68 × 100 = _____

30. 5.095 × 100 = _____

31. 100 × 50.95 = _____

Multiply.

32. 1.8 × 1,000 = _____

33. 2.1 × 1,000 = _____

34. 9.097 × 1,000 = _____

35. 1,000 × 7.007 = _____

36. 2.74 × 1,000 = _____

37. 27.4 × 1,000 = _____

38. 1,000 × 10.81 = _____

39. 108.1 × 1,000 = _____

Complete.

Example
1.2 = 0.12 × ___10___
    = 0.012 × ___100___

40. 360 = 36 × _____

= 3.6 × _____

= 0.36 × _____

41. 438 = _____ × 10

= _____ × 100

= _____ × 1,000

42. 7,256 = _____ × 10

= _____ × 100

= _____ × 1,000

Multiply.

Example

$$0.3 \times 700 = (0.3 \times 7) \times 100$$
$$= \underline{\quad 2.1 \quad} \times 100 = \underline{\quad 210 \quad}$$

So, $0.3 \times 700 = \underline{\quad 210 \quad}$.

43. $0.003 \times 700 = (0.003 \times \underline{\qquad}) \times 100$
$$= \underline{\qquad} \times 100 = \underline{\qquad}$$

So, $0.003 \times 700 = \underline{\qquad}$.

44. $0.03 \times 2,000 = (0.03 \times \underline{\qquad}) \times 1,000$
$$= \underline{\qquad} \times 1,000 = \underline{\qquad}$$

So, $0.03 \times 2,000 = \underline{\qquad}$.

45. $0.003 \times 2,000 = (0.003 \times \underline{\qquad}) \times 1,000$
$$= \underline{\qquad} \times 1,000 = \underline{\qquad}$$

So, $0.003 \times 2,000 = \underline{\qquad}$.

Find each product.

46. $4.5 \times 200 = \underline{\qquad}$ **47.** $0.49 \times 300 = \underline{\qquad}$

48. $3.148 \times 500 = \underline{\qquad}$ **49.** $2.27 \times 700 = \underline{\qquad}$

50. $900 \times 3.18 = \underline{\qquad}$ **51.** $1.8 \times 2,000 = \underline{\qquad}$

52. $4,000 \times 2.5 = \underline{\qquad}$ **53.** $72.5 \times 6,000 = \underline{\qquad}$

54. $1.75 \times 8,000 = \underline{\qquad}$ **55.** $4.19 \times 9,000 = \underline{\qquad}$

Practice 3 Dividing Decimals

Divide. Write the quotient as a decimal.

Example

0.6 ÷ 2 = _____6_____ tenths ÷ 2

= _____3_____ tenths

= __0.3__

So, 0.6 ÷ 2 = __0.3__.

1. 0.8 ÷ 4 = _____ tenths ÷ 4

= _____ tenths

= _____

So, 0.8 ÷ 4 = _____.

2. 1 ÷ 5 = _____ tenths ÷ 5

= _____ tenths

= _____

So, 1 ÷ 5 = _____.

3. 2.4 ÷ 6 = _____ tenths ÷ 6

= _____ tenths

= _____

So, 2.4 ÷ 6 = _____.

Complete. Write the quotient as a decimal.

Example

$0.08 \div 2 =$ ___8___ hundredths $\div$ ___2___

$=$ ___4___ hundredths

$=$ ___0.04___

So, $0.08 \div 2 =$ ___0.04___.

---

4. $0.14 \div 7 =$ _____ hundredths $\div$ _____

$=$ _____ hundredths

$=$ _____

So, $0.14 \div 7 =$ _____.

5. $0.27 \div 9 =$ _____ hundredths $\div$ _____

$=$ _____ hundredths

$=$ _____

So, $0.27 \div 9 =$ _____.

6. $0.1 \div 2 =$ _____ hundredths $\div$ _____

$=$ _____ hundredths

$=$ _____

So, $0.1 \div 2 =$ _____.

Divide. Round each quotient to the nearest tenth.

Example

$7 \div 8$

```
      0.87
  8) 7.00
     0
     ──
     7 0
     6 4
     ────
       6 0
       5 6
       ────
         4
```

First, divide to two decimal places. Then round the answer to the nearest tenth.

$7 \div 8$ is about 0.9.

21. $5 \div 7$

```
7) 5
```

22. $11 \div 9$

```
9) 1 1
```

Divide. Round each quotient to the nearest hundredth.

Example

$14.7 \div 9$

```
        1. 6 3 3
  9) 1 4. 7 0 0
      9
      ‾‾‾‾
      5 7
      5 4
      ‾‾‾‾
        3 0
        2 7
        ‾‾‾‾
          3 0
          2 7
          ‾‾‾‾
            3
```

First, divide to three decimal places. Then round the answer to the nearest hundredth.

$14.7 \div 9$ is about 1.63.

---

23. $3.2 \div 7$

```
  7) 3 . 2
```

24. $13 \div 6$

```
  6) 1   3
```

Divide.

17.   4.8 ÷ 20 = _____

18.   0.32 ÷ 40 = _____

19.   2.08 ÷ 80 = _____

20.   2.55 ÷ 50 = _____

21.   3.5 ÷ 70 = _____

22.   0.3 ÷ 60 = _____

Divide.

23.   7.5 ÷ 100 = _____

24.   49.3 ÷ 100 = _____

25.   6,001 ÷ 100 = _____

26.   708.2 ÷ 100 = _____

27.   900 ÷ 1,000 = _____

28.   4,103 ÷ 1,000 = _____

29.   909 ÷ 1,000 = _____

30.   9,009 ÷ 1,000 = _____

Complete.

31.   86.2 ÷ _____ = 0.862

32.   275 ÷ _____ = 0.275

33.   _____ ÷ 100 = 0.006

34.   _____ ÷ 1,000 = 3.082

Complete.

> **Example**
>
> 0.07 = 0.7 ÷ _10_
>
>   = 7 ÷ _100_
>
>   = 70 ÷ _1,000_

35.   0.31 = 3.1 ÷ _____

           = 31 ÷ _____

           = 310 ÷ _____

36.   8.06 = _____ ÷ 10

           = 806 ÷ _____

           = 8,060 ÷ _____

37.   5.115 = _____ ÷ 10

           = _____ ÷ 100

           = 5,115 ÷ _____

Complete.

$42 \div 200 = (42 \div \underline{2}) \div 100$

$= \underline{21} \div 100$

$= \underline{0.21}$

So, $42 \div 200 = \underline{0.21}$.

38. $18.9 \div 900 = (18.9 \div \underline{}) \div 100$

$= \underline{} \div 100$

$= \underline{}$

So, $18.9 \div 900 = \underline{}$.

39. $2 \div 2{,}000 = (2 \div \underline{}) \div 1{,}000$

$= \underline{} \div 1{,}000$

$= \underline{}$

So, $2 \div 2{,}000 = \underline{}$.

40. $1{,}500 \div 6{,}000 = (1{,}500 \div \underline{}) \div 1{,}000$

$= \underline{} \div 1{,}000$

$= \underline{}$

So, $1{,}500 \div 6{,}000 = \underline{}$.

Divide.

41. $306 \div 600 = \underline{}$

42. $29.7 \div 900 = \underline{}$

43. $1{,}056 \div 800 = \underline{}$

44. $48 \div 2{,}000 = \underline{}$

45. $408 \div 3{,}000 = \underline{}$

46. $805 \div 7{,}000 = \underline{}$

Practice 5   Estimating Decimals

Round each decimal to the nearest whole number.
Then estimate the sum or difference.

Example

7.7 + 12.3

7.7 rounds to 8.
12.3 rounds to 12.
8 + 12 = 20
7.7 + 12.3 is about 20.

21.8 − 11.5

21.8 rounds to 22.
11.5 rounds to 12.
22 − 12 = 10
21.8 − 11.5 is about 10.

1. $2.90 + $7.15

2.   9.05 + 19.55

3.   35.67 − 15.09

4. $15.40 − $5.95

Estimate the product by rounding the decimal to the nearest whole number.

Example

4.5 × 4

4.5 rounds to 5.
5 × 4 = 20

4.5 × 4 is about 20.

5. 19.6 × 3

6. 0.95 × 8

7. 8.25 × 3

Estimate the quotient by choosing a whole number close to the dividend that can be evenly divided by the divisor.

Example

24.6 ÷ 5

24.6 is about 25.
25 ÷ 5 = 5

24.6 ÷ 5 is about 5.

8. 38.4 ÷ 6

9. 71.09 ÷ 8

10. 99.75 ÷ 5

© Marshall Cavendish International (Singapore) Private Limited.

Round each decimal to the nearest tenth. Then estimate.

11.   0.47 + 15.51

12.   9.95 − 1.46

13.   2.89 pounds × 4

Estimate the quotient by choosing a tenth close to the dividend that can be evenly divided by the divisor.

14.   6.34 kilograms ÷ 7

Solve. Show your work.

15. A bag of walnuts sells for $1.95. Estimate the cost of 8 bags of walnuts.

16. A piece of plywood is 1.27 centimeters thick. Find the thickness of a pile of 9 pieces of plywood to the nearest tenth of a centimeter. Estimate to check if your answer is reasonable.

Solve. Show your work.

7. During the summer, Andrew worked for 6 days each week. He worked 8 hours each day. In a week, he earned $360. How much was he paid for each hour of work?

8. A bag contains 10 pounds of dog food. A family feeds their dogs 0.85 pound of dog food a day. How much dog food is left in the bag after 7 days? Give your answer to the nearest pound.

Solve. Show your work.

9. A box of rice cakes costs $1.95. What is the greatest number of boxes of rice cakes Jared can buy with $10?

10. A metal rod 9.4 meters long is cut into two pieces. One piece is 3 times as long as the other. Find the length of the longer piece in meters. Round your answer to the nearest tenth of a meter.

Solve. Show your work.

11. Rani bought 9 similar notebooks. She gave the cashier $10 and received change of $5.05. What was the cost of 1 notebook?

12. A kilogram of whole-wheat flour costs $6. What is the cost of 400 grams of the flour?

Solve. Show your work.

13. A shop owner bought 30 folders and some journals. He paid $82.50 for the folders. Each journal cost 10 times as much as a folder. What was the cost of each journal?

14. There are 1,000 workers in a factory. Each worker works 30 hours a week and is paid $10.50 an hour. How much does the company pay the workers altogether each week?

Practice 7 Real-World Problems: Decimals

Solve. Show your work.

1. Mrs. Lee uses 0.025 kilogram of wax to make a candle.
    On Monday, she made 50 candles. On Tuesday, she made 4 times as
    many candles as on Monday. How much wax did she use to make the
    candles on Tuesday?

2. One lap of a race track measures 4.68 kilometers. During a race of
    56 laps, a driver stops to refuel after completing 48 laps. How many
    more kilometers does he have to drive to finish the race?

Solve. Show your work.

3. Mrs. Rahlee bought 300 yards of ribbon to make flowers. She used 1.22 yards to make one large flower. She made 200 such large flowers She used all of the remaining ribbon to make 100 small flowers. What was the length of ribbon Mrs. Rahlee used to make one small flower?

4. Britta bought some carrots and apples for $24.80. A carrot and an apple cost $0.90 altogether. She bought more carrots than apples. The cost of the extra number of carrots was $6.80. How many apples did Britta buy?

Solve. Show your work.

5. A plastic tub has a capacity of 13.5 quarts. It can hold 3 times as much
    liquid as a pail. The pail can hold twice as much liquid as a can.
    Find the capacity of the pail and that of the can in quarts.

6. Marcy paid $35 for 10 kilograms of raisins. She divided the raisins equally
    into two containers. Then she sold the raisins in the first container at $4.50
    per kilogram and those in the second container at $5.50 per kilogram.
    How much money did Marcy earn after selling all the raisins?

 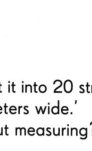

Math Journal

Solve. Show your work.

1. James has a square piece of paper. He wants to cut it into 20 strips of equal width.
He says, 'This piece of paper is **about** 48 centimeters wide.'
How can he find out the width of each strip without measuring?
Is this width accurate?

2. James takes a ruler and measures the width of the piece of paper.
He finds that the actual width is 48.8 centimeters.
Find the width of each strip. How can you check if your answer
is reasonable?

Put On Your Thinking Cap!

Challenging Practice

Solve. Show your work.

1. A plumber has two pipes. One pipe is 7 times as long as the other pipe. He cuts 2.2 meters from the longer pipe. The remaining length of this pipe is 3 times that of the shorter pipe. Find the length of the shorter pipe in meters.

2. At a farmer's market, 5 pounds of strawberries cost $21.50. At a supermarket, 3 pounds of the same quality strawberries cost $15.75.

   a. Which is a better buy?

   b. How much can you save by buying 20 pounds of the strawberries that are the better buy?

Put On Your Thinking Cap!

Problem Solving

Solve. Show your work.

1. Sam buys 10 oranges and 11 apples for $10.05. The total cost of 1 orange and 1 apple is $0.94. How much does an apple cost?

2. A bucket filled with sand has a mass of 11.15 kilograms. When it is filled with water, the mass is 5.95 kilograms. The mass of the sand is twice that of the water. Find the mass of the bucket in grams.

Solve. Show your work.

3.   The total capacity of 6 pitchers and 12 glasses is 21 liters. The capacity
of a pitcher is 5 times that of a glass. Find the capacity of each glass.
Give your answer in liters.

Solve. Show your work.

4. Dahlia has just enough money to buy either 6 pears and 20 oranges or 12 oranges and 11 pears. A pear costs $0.80. How much does an orange cost?

Chapter 10 Percent

Practice 1 Percent

**Each large square is divided into 100 parts.
Fill in the blanks to describe each large square.**

1.

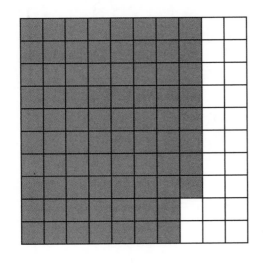

_____ out of 100 equal parts are shaded.

_____% of the large square is shaded.

_____ out of 100 equal parts are not shaded.

_____% of the large square is not shaded.

2.

_____ out of 100 equal parts are shaded.

_____% of the large square is shaded.

_____ out of 100 equal parts are not shaded.

_____% of the large square is not shaded.

Express each fraction as a percent.

> **Example**
>
> $\dfrac{38}{100} = $ _____38_____ %

3. $\dfrac{92}{100} = $ _____ %

4. $\dfrac{7}{100} = $ _____ %

5. $\dfrac{19}{100} = $ _____ %

6. $\dfrac{6}{10} = $ _____ %

7. $\dfrac{4}{10} = $ _____ %

Express each decimal as a percent.

> **Example**
>
> $0.15 = \dfrac{\boxed{15}}{100}$
>
> $= $ _____15_____ %

8. $0.28 = \dfrac{\boxed{}}{100}$

$= $ _____ %

9. $0.07 = $ _____ %

10. $0.01 = $ _____ %

11. $0.08 = $ _____ %

12. $0.5 = $ _____ %

13. $0.9 = $ _____ %

14. $0.8 = $ _____ %

Express each percent as a fraction with a denominator of 100.

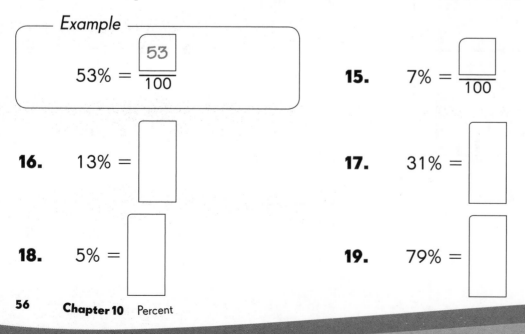

> **Example**
>
> $53\% = \dfrac{\boxed{53}}{100}$

15. $7\% = \dfrac{\boxed{}}{100}$

16. $13\% = \boxed{}$

17. $31\% = \boxed{}$

18. $5\% = \boxed{}$

19. $79\% = \boxed{}$

Express each percent as a fraction in simplest form.

Example

$$5\% = \dfrac{5}{100}$$

$$= \dfrac{1}{20}$$

20. $25\% = \dfrac{\boxed{}}{100}$

$= \boxed{}$

21. $75\% = \boxed{}$

22. $84\% = \boxed{}$

23. $46\% = \boxed{}$

24. $55\% = \boxed{}$

Express each percent as a decimal.

Example

$$27\% = \dfrac{27}{100}$$

$$= \underline{\quad 0.27 \quad}$$

25. $58\% = \dfrac{\boxed{}}{100}$

$= \underline{\qquad\qquad}$

26. $9\% = \underline{\qquad\qquad}$

27. $1\% = \underline{\qquad\qquad}$

Write each ratio as a fraction and then as a percent.

		As a Fraction	As a Percent
28.	23 out of 100		
29.	9 out of 10		

Express each percent as a decimal. Then mark X to show where each decimal is located on the number line.

30.   71% = _____   **31.**   19% = _____   **32.**   44% = _____

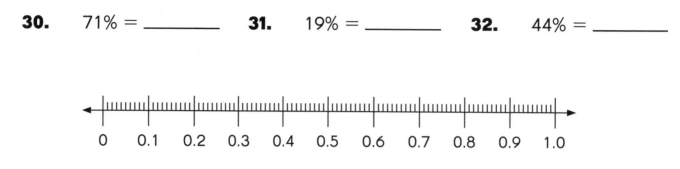

Solve. Show your work.

33.   There are 100 students in a drawing contest, and 58 of them are girls.

   a.   What percent of the students in the contest are girls?

   b.   What percent of the students in the contest are boys?

34.   A jogging route is 10 kilometers long. Lee Ming has jogged 4 kilometers of the route.

   a.   What percent of the route has Lee Ming jogged?

   b.   What percent of the route does Lee Ming have to jog to complete the whole route?

Practice 2 Expressing Fractions as Percents

Express each fraction as a percent.

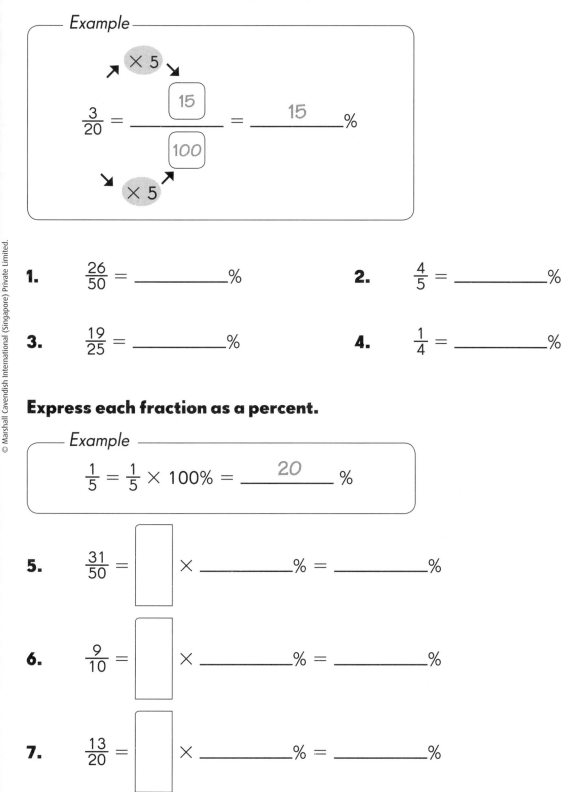

Example

$$\frac{3}{20} = \frac{\boxed{15}}{\boxed{100}} = \underline{\hspace{1cm}15\hspace{1cm}}\%$$

×5

×5

1. $\frac{26}{50} = \underline{\hspace{1.5cm}}\%$

2. $\frac{4}{5} = \underline{\hspace{1.5cm}}\%$

3. $\frac{19}{25} = \underline{\hspace{1.5cm}}\%$

4. $\frac{1}{4} = \underline{\hspace{1.5cm}}\%$

Express each fraction as a percent.

Example

$$\frac{1}{5} = \frac{1}{5} \times 100\% = \underline{\hspace{1cm}20\hspace{1cm}}\%$$

5. $\frac{31}{50} = \boxed{} \times \underline{\hspace{1.5cm}}\% = \underline{\hspace{1.5cm}}\%$

6. $\frac{9}{10} = \boxed{} \times \underline{\hspace{1.5cm}}\% = \underline{\hspace{1.5cm}}\%$

7. $\frac{13}{20} = \boxed{} \times \underline{\hspace{1.5cm}}\% = \underline{\hspace{1.5cm}}\%$

Express each fraction as a percent.
Use the model to help you.

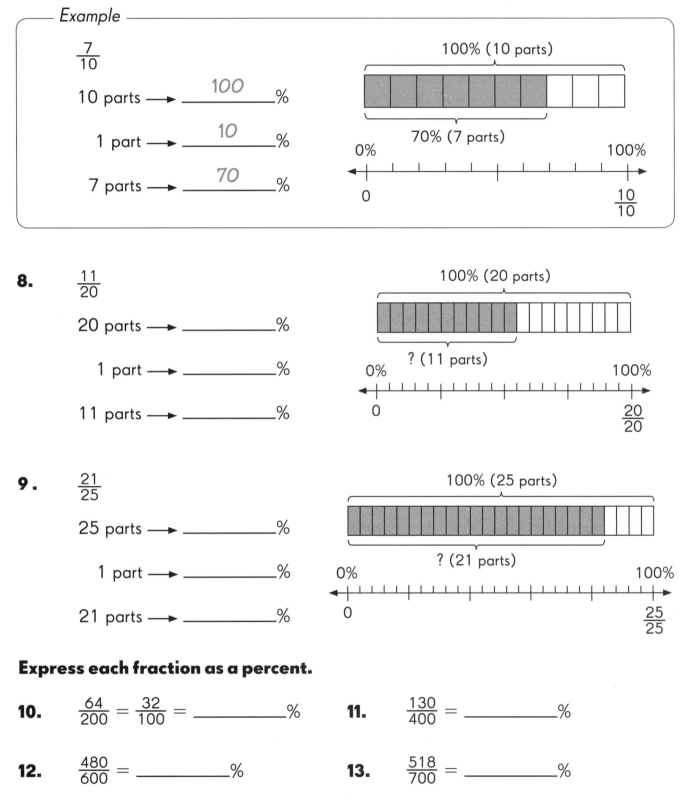

Example

$\frac{7}{10}$

10 parts ⟶ _100_ %

1 part ⟶ _10_ %

7 parts ⟶ _70_ %

100% (10 parts)

70% (7 parts)

0%   100%

0                    $\frac{10}{10}$

---

8. $\frac{11}{20}$

20 parts ⟶ _____ %

1 part ⟶ _____ %

11 parts ⟶ _____ %

100% (20 parts)

? (11 parts)

0%   100%

0                    $\frac{20}{20}$

---

9. $\frac{21}{25}$

25 parts ⟶ _____ %

1 part ⟶ _____ %

21 parts ⟶ _____ %

100% (25 parts)

? (21 parts)

0%   100%

0                    $\frac{25}{25}$

Express each fraction as a percent.

10. $\frac{64}{200} = \frac{32}{100} =$ _____ %

11. $\frac{130}{400} =$ _____ %

12. $\frac{480}{600} =$ _____ %

13. $\frac{518}{700} =$ _____ %

Solve. Show your work.

14. Jeremy finished $\frac{3}{5}$ of his homework. What percent of his homework did he finish?

15. Tracy ran in a marathon, but managed to complete only $\frac{13}{20}$ of the race.

   a. What percent of the marathon did she complete?

   b. What percent of the marathon did she not complete?

Solve. Show your work.

16. Katie bought some flour. She used $\frac{3}{8}$ of it to bake bread.

What percent of the flour is left?

17. There are 800 members in an astronomy club, and 320 of them are females. What percent of the members are males?

Practice 3   Percent of a Number

Multiply.

1.   25% × 84 = _____

2.   36% × 75 = _____

3.   40% of 680 = _____

4.   55% of 720 = _____

Solve. Show your work.

5.   Of the 240 shirts on a rack, 40% are size medium.
How many shirts on the rack are size medium?

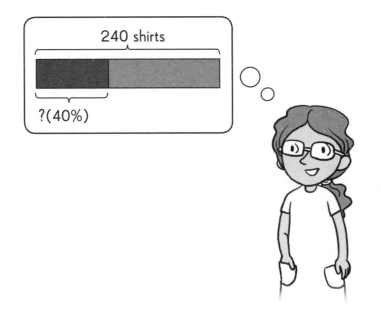

Solve. Show your work.

6. There are 720 students in a school. One rainy day, 5% of the students were absent. How many students were absent?

5% of 720 = ?

7. Jenny made 200 bracelets. She sold 64% of the bracelets at a craft fair.

    a. How many bracelets did she sell?

    b. How many bracelets were not sold?

Solve. Show your work.

8. There were 12,000 spectators in one section of the stadium. In that section, 55% had on red shirts and the rest had on white shirts. How many spectators had on white shirts?

9. Mrs. Patel went shopping with $120. She spent 12% of the money on meat, and 25% on vegetables. How much money did she have left?

Solve. Show your work.

10. A vendor sells three types of watches. Of the watches in stock, 20% are men's watches, 40% are ladies' watches and the rest are children's watches. There are 250 watches altogether. How many children's watches are there?

Practice 4 Real-World Problems: Percent

Solve. Show your work.

1. Jennifer bought a printer that cost $240. There was a 7% sales tax on the printer.

   a. How much sales tax did Jennifer pay?

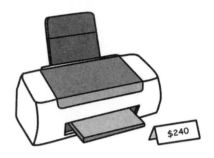

$240

   b. How much did Jennifer pay for the printer with tax?

2. A company invests $8,000 in an account that pays 6% interest per year.

   a. How much interest will the company earn at the end of 1 year?

   b. How much money will the company have in the account at the
   end of 1 year?

Solve. Show your work.

3.   The regular price of a digital camera was $250. Tyrone bought the digital camera at a discount of 40%. How much did Tyrone pay for the digital camera?

4.   Len bought a new car for $22,500. After a few years, he sold the car at a discount of 25%. What was the selling price of the car?

Solve. Show your work.

5. The price for dinner in a restaurant was $80. The customer paid an additional 7% meals tax and left a $15 tip.

   a. How much meals tax did the customer pay?

   b. How much did the customer spend altogether in the restaurant?

6. The regular price of a pair of hockey skates was $250. Ron bought the skates at a discount of 8%. However, he had to pay 5% sales tax on the skates after the discount.

   a. What was the selling price of the skates?

   b. How much did Ron pay for the skates in total?

Math Journal

Arnold had dinner at a restaurant with his family. The dinner cost $72. In addition, he paid 7% meals tax on the dinner. How much did Arnold pay for the dinner?

Tyrone worked out the answer using his calculator like this:

$$93\% \times \$72 = \$66.96$$

Brandon worked out the answer using his calculator like this:

$$107\% \times \$72 = \$77.04$$

Whose answer is correct? Explain why his answer is correct.

Put On Your Thinking Cap!

Challenging Practice

Solve. Show your work.

1. Mr. Stanton bought a cell phone at 80% of the regular price. The regular price of the phone was $450. Mr. Wilson bought the same cell phone but paid $500 for it. How much more did Mr. Wilson pay than Mr. Stanton?

2. Helen has 30 tickets. Gina has 20 more tickets than Helen. What percent of her tickets must Gina give Helen so that both of them have the same number of tickets?

Put On Your Thinking Cap!

Problem Solving

Solve. Show your work.

Michelle collects U.S., Canadian, and Mexican stamps. In her collection, 80% of the stamps are U.S. and Mexican stamps. There are 3 times as many U.S. stamps as Mexican stamps. What percent of Michelle's collection is made up of U.S. stamps?

Cumulative Review

for Chapters 8 to 10

Concepts and Skills

Mark X to show where each decimal is located on the number line. *(Lesson 8.1)*

1.   0.032   **2.**   0.047

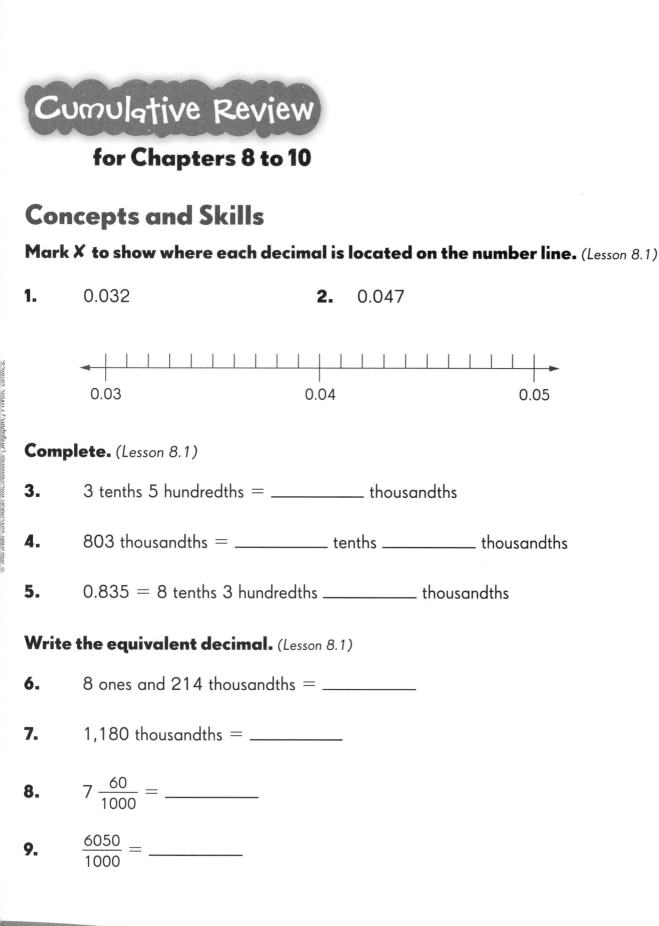

Complete. *(Lesson 8.1)*

3.   3 tenths 5 hundredths = _____ thousandths

4.   803 thousandths = _____ tenths _____ thousandths

5.   0.835 = 8 tenths 3 hundredths _____ thousandths

Write the equivalent decimal. *(Lesson 8.1)*

6.   8 ones and 214 thousandths = _____

7.   1,180 thousandths = _____

8. $7\frac{60}{1000}$ = _____

9. $\frac{6050}{1000}$ = _____

4.526 can be written in expanded form as 4 + 0.5 + 0.02 + 0.006. Write each decimal in expanded notation. *(Lesson 8.1)*

10. 0.329 = _____ + _____ + _____

11. 20.125 = _____ + _____ + _____ + _____

Complete. *(Lesson 8.1)*

In 9.168,

12. the digit 6 is in the _____ place.

13. the value of the digit 8 is _____.

14. the digit 1 stands for _____.

Compare. Write >, <, or =. *(Lesson 8.2)*

15. 1.07 ◯ 1.7

16. 3.562 ◯ 3.526

17. 15.4 ◯ 15.40

Order the decimals. *(Lesson 8.2)*

18. 2.08,   1.973,   6.1

Begin with the least:

_____

19. 1.567,   1.667,   1.376

Begin with the greatest:

_____

Fill in the blanks. *(Lesson 8.2)*

20. The mass of a strand of hair is 0.179 gram.

Round the mass to the nearest hundredth of a gram.

0.179 gram rounds to _____ gram.

21. The length of a rope is 2.589 yards.

Round the length to the nearest tenth of a yard.

2.589 yards rounds to _____ yards.

Write each decimal as a mixed number in simplest form. *(Lesson 8.3)*

22. $6.2 =$ _____

23. $2.16 =$ _____

Multiply. *(Lessons 9.1 and 9.2)*

24. $29.3 \times 8 =$ _____

25. $12.08 \times 5 =$ _____

26. $86.4 \times 10 =$ _____

27. $13.5 \times 30 =$ _____

28. $73.96 \times 100 =$ _____

29. $6.2 \times 700 =$ _____

30. $9.34 \times 1,000 =$ _____

31. $25.6 \times 9,000 =$ _____

Divide. (*Lesson 9.3*)

32. $0.5 \div 5 =$ _____

33. $0.63 \div 9 =$ _____

34. $36.8 \div 4 =$ _____

35. $96.3 \div 5 =$ _____

36. $3.36 \div 4 =$ _____

37. $1.92 \div 8 =$ _____

Divide. Round the quotient to the nearest tenth and nearest hundredth. (*Lesson 9.3*)

38. $19 \div 7 =$ _____ to the nearest tenth

$19 \div 7 =$ _____ to the nearest hundredth

Divide. (Lesson 9.4)

39. 38 ÷ 10 = _____

40. 19.6 ÷ 20 = _____

41. 4.5 ÷ 100 = _____

42. 375 ÷ 300 = _____

43. 5,030 ÷ 1,000 = _____

44. 2,506 ÷ 7,000 = _____

Estimate each answer by rounding the numbers to an appropriate place. (Lesson 9.5)

45. 91.2 + 25.9

46. 37.4 − 11.7

47. 21.63 × 5

48. 7.05 ÷ 8

Write each ratio in three ways. Complete the table. *(Lesson 10.1)*

		As a Fraction	As a Percent	As a Decimal
49.	57 out of 100			
50.	8 out of 10			

Express each fraction as a percent. *(Lesson 10.2)*

51. $\dfrac{88}{200} =$

52. $\dfrac{204}{400} =$

53. $\dfrac{6}{20} =$

54. $\dfrac{7}{50} =$

55. $\dfrac{13}{20} =$

56. $\dfrac{16}{25} =$

Problem Solving

Solve.

57.   Hazel saves $5.75 each week.

   a. How much does she save in 2 weeks?

   b. She spends $23.83 on a book and $9.12 on a wallet. How much does she spend on the two items?

58.   Evelyn has 12.7 quarts of fruit punch in a cooler. She pours the fruit punch into glasses. She fills 5 glasses, each with a capacity of 0.36 quart. Then she fills 8 glasses, each with a capacity of 0.52 quart. How much fruit punch is left in the cooler?

Solve. Use models to help you.

59. The total weight of three tables is 16.9 pounds. The first table is twice as heavy as the second table. The weight of the third table is $\frac{1}{3}$ the weight of the second table. What is the weight of the first table?

60. There are 950 seats in a theater. 82% of the seats are occupied. How many seats are not occupied?

Solve. Use models to help you.

61. Rahul spends 10% of his weekly allowance on Monday. On Wednesday, he spends $\frac{1}{3}$ of the remainder. What percent of his allowance is left at the end of Wednesday?

62. Ms. Jones buys a violin for $860. In addition, she has to pay 7% sales tax. How much does she pay in all?

Solve.

63. The regular price of a television set is $1,200. Albert buys the television set at a discount of 35%. How much does he pay for the television set?

64. A school band gives a year-end concert. It is held in a 400-seat auditorium. Each concert ticket sells for $10, and 85% of the tickets are sold. How much money does the band earn from the sale of the tickets?

Chapter 11 Graphs and Probability

Practice 1 Making and Interpreting Double Bar Graphs

Complete. Use the data in the graph.

The double bar graph shows the number of boys and girls in two classes, 5A and 5B.

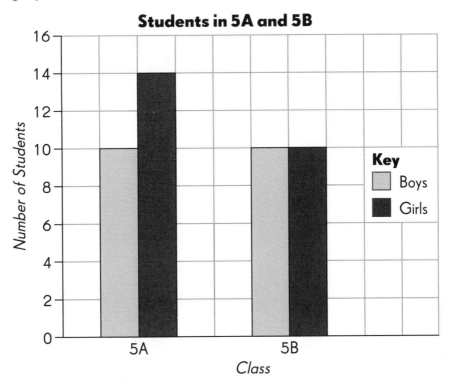

Students in 5A and 5B

Key
Boys
Girls

Number of Students

Class

1. There are _____ students in 5A and _____ students in 5B.

2. There are _____ more girls than boys in 5A.

3. Class _____ has an equal number of boys and girls.

4. There are _____ girls altogether in 5A and 5B.

5. There are _____ boys altogether in 5A and 5B.

6. The average number of students in the two classes is _____.

Complete the bar graph using the data in the table. Then answer the questions.

7. The table shows the number of bags of apples and oranges sold by a grocer on three days.

	Thursday	Friday	Saturday
Number of Bags of Apples	20	25	30
Number of Bags of Oranges	25	35	45

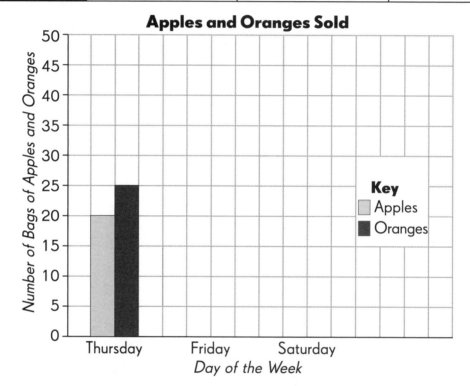

8. On Friday, _____ more bags of oranges than apples were sold.

9. On Saturday, _____ fewer bags of apples than oranges were sold.

10. The total number of bags of apples and oranges sold was the greatest on

_____.

11. The difference between the number of bags of apples and oranges sold

was the least on _____.

Name: _Ethan R._ Date: _12/15/14_

Practice 2 Graphing an Equation

Write the ordered pair for each point.

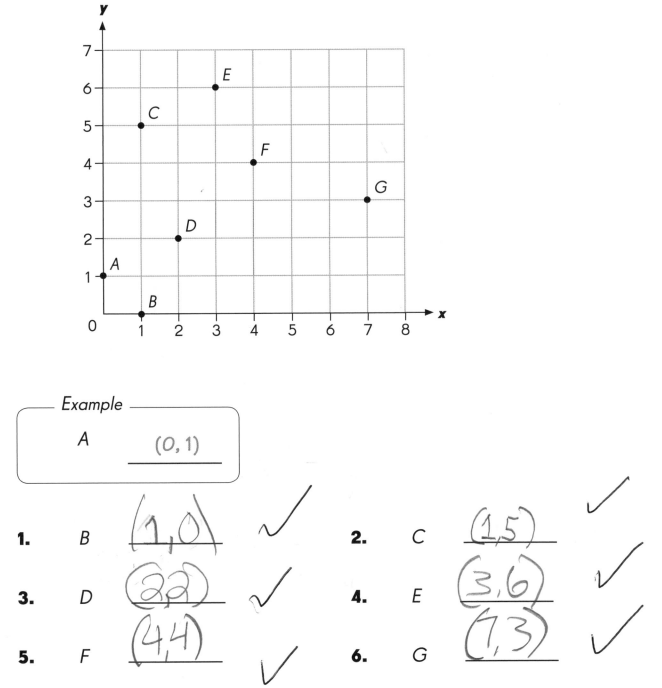

Example

A _(0, 1)_

1. B (1, 0) ✓

2. C (1, 5) ✓

3. D (2, 2) ✓

4. E (3, 6) ✓

5. F (4, 4) ✓

6. G (7, 3) ✓

Plot each point on the coordinate grid.

7. $P(0, 5)$ **8.** $Q(4, 0)$

9. $R(3, 6)$ **10.** $S(5, 1)$

11. $T(2, 5)$ **12.** $U(0, 0)$

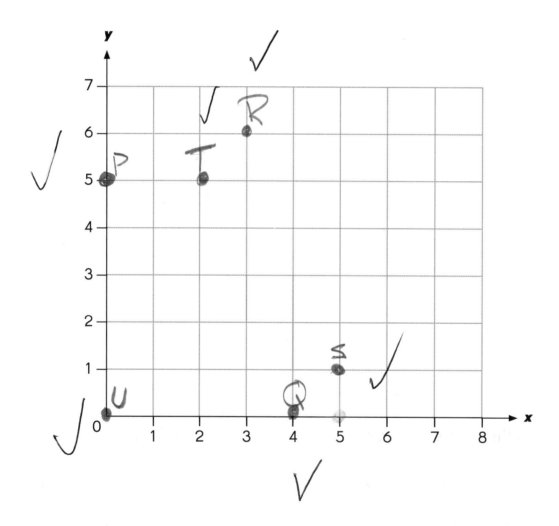

Use the graph to answer the questions.

The perimeter of a square is P centimeters and the length of each side is s centimeters. A graph of $P = 4s$ is drawn.

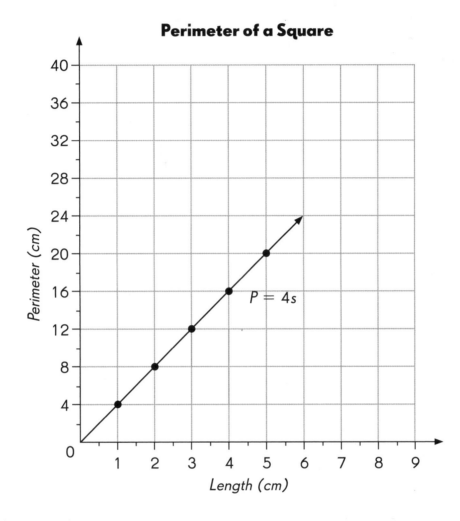

Perimeter of a Square

Perimeter (cm)

$P = 4s$

Length (cm)

13. What is the perimeter of a square of side 2 centimeters? _____

14. What is the perimeter of a square of side 4.5 centimeters? _____

15. What is the length of a side of a square if its perimeter is 4 centimeters? _____

16. What is the length of a side of a square if its perimeter is 10 centimeters? _____

17. If the point (7, M) is on the graph what is the value of M? _____

Complete the table.

18. Each bottle contains 2 liters of cooking oil.

Number of Bottles (*x*)	1	2	3		5	6
Number of Liters (*y*)	2		6	8		12

Complete the graph using the data in the table. Then answer the questions.

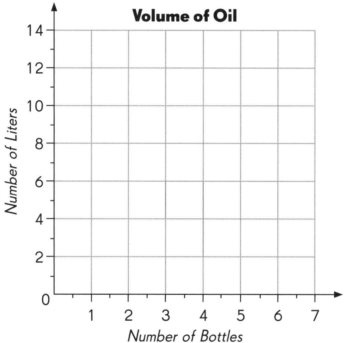

19. How many liters of oil are in 3 bottles? _____

20. How many liters of oil are in 2.5 bottles? _____

21. How many bottles contain 8 liters of oil? _____

22. How many bottles contain 7 liters of oil? _____

23. How many bottles contain 11 liters of oil? _____

Practice 3   Combinations

Complete.

A bag has 1 red, 1 blue, and 1 green marble. Another bag has 1 red and 1 blue cube.

1.   List all the possible combinations of choosing 1 marble and 1 cube.

Color of Marble	Color of Cube

2.   There are _____ combinations.

Complete.

In a soccer tournament, there are two groups. Each group has three teams.
Teams A, B, and C are in Group 1. Teams X, Y, and Z are in Group 2.
Each team in Group 1 plays against every team in Group 2.

3.   Complete the table for the games played.

		Group 1		
		A	**B**	**C**
Group 2	**X**			
	Y			
	Z			

4.   The number of combinations of games for the six teams is _____.

Draw a tree diagram to find the number of combinations.

5.   Ms. Li has 4 different books and 1 red pen, 1 blue pen, and 1 black pen.
         She is wrapping one book and one pen to give as a gift.
         Draw a tree diagram to find the number of combinations she can choose.

There are _____ combinations.

Find the number of combinations.

6.   Rina has 1 black, 1 red, and 1 yellow skirt.
           She has 1 white, 1 floral, and 1 striped shirt.

    a.   Draw a tree diagram to show the possible outfits Rina can wear.

    b.   Find the number of outfits by multiplication.

       The number of outfits is _____.

Complete.

7. There are 4 colors on a spinner. There are 6 faces on a number cube, numbered 1 to 6. The spinner is spun and the number cube is tossed.

There are _____ combinations of color and number.

8. A bookshelf has 10 mathematics books, 8 science books, and 12 history books.

a. There are _____ combinations of a mathematics book and a science book.

b. There are _____ combinations of a science book and a history book.

c. There are _____ combinations of a mathematics book and a history book.

Practice 4 Theoretical Probability and Experimental Probability

Use the table to answer the questions.
Express each probability as a decimal.

A spinner has four equal sections in four different colors, red, blue, green, and yellow. The spinner is spun 100 times. The table shows the number of times it lands on each color.

Outcome	Number of Times
lands on red	28
lands on blue	25
lands on green	24
lands on yellow	23

1. What is the experimental probability of landing on red?

_____

2. What is the experimental probability of landing on blue?

_____

3. What is the experimental probability of landing on green?

_____

4. What is the experimental probability of landing on yellow?

_____

5. What is the theoretical probability of landing on each of the four colors?

_____

Use the table to answer the questions.
Express each probability as a fraction is simplest form.

A number cube has 1 face numbered 1, 2 faces numbered 2,
and 3 faces numbered 3. The cube is tossed 100 times.
The table shows the number of times each number is shown.

Outcome	Number of Times
cube shows 1	14
cube shows 2	34
cube shows 3	52

6.   What is the experimental probability of the cube showing 1?

_____

7.   What is the theoretical probability of the cube showing 1?

_____

8.   What is the experimental probability of the cube showing 2?

_____

9.   What is the theoretical probability of the cube showing 2?

_____

10.   What is the experimental probability of the cube showing 3?

_____

11.   What is the theoretical probability of the cube showing 3?

_____

Use the table to answer the questions.
Express each probability as a decimal.

A bag contains 2 blue marbles, 3 red marbles, and 5 green marbles.
A marble is drawn from the bag, its color is noted and the marble is returned
to the bag. The table shows the results of drawing a marble 200 times.

Outcome	Number of Times
blue marble	36
red marble	56
green marble	108

12. What is the experimental probability of drawing a blue marble?

_____

13. What is the theoretical probability of drawing a blue marble?

_____

14. What is the experimental probability of drawing a red marble?

_____

15. What is the theoretical probability of drawing a red marble?

_____

16. What is the experimental probability of drawing a green marble?

_____

17. What is the theoretical probability of drawing a green marble?

_____

Complete.

A spinner is divided into 16 equal parts. Each part is colored green, yellow, or blue. The spinner is spun 25 times. The tally chart shows the number of times it lands on each color.

Color	Tally	Number
green	////	4
yellow	~~////~~ ////	9
blue	~~////~~ ~~////~~ //	12

18. Which is the likely set of colors on the spinner, Set A, Set B, or Set C?

Set _____

	Green	Yellow	Blue
Set A	3	10	3
Set B	6	5	5
Set C	2	6	8

19. What is the experimental probability of landing on green?

_____

20. What is the experimental probability of landing on yellow?

_____

21. What is the experimental probability of landing on blue?

_____

Name: _____   Date: _____

Put On Your Thinking Cap!

Challenging Practice

Complete.

1. The table shows the conversion from gallons to pints. Complete the table.

Number of Gallons (x)	1	2	3	4	5	6
Number of Pints (y)		16			40	

2. Write the equation relating the number of pints (y) to the number of gallons (x).

_____

3. Draw the graph of the equation. Label the axes and the equation.

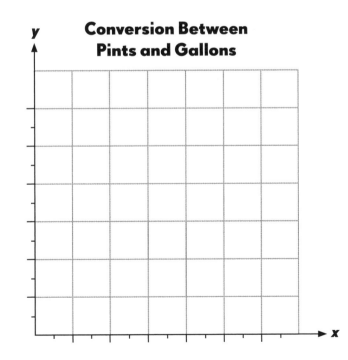

Conversion Between Pints and Gallons

Use the graph to answer the questions.

4. How many pints is $3\frac{1}{2}$ gallons?

5. How many pints is $4\frac{1}{2}$ gallons?

6. How many gallons is 20 pints?

7. How many gallons is 44 pints?

Complete.

8. The table shows the conversion from quarts to cups. Complete the table.

Number of Quarts (x)	1	2	3			6
Number of Cups (y)		8		16	20	24

9. Write the equation relating the number of cups (y) to the number of quarts (x).

_____

Put On Your Thinking Cap!

Problem Solving

Solve.

1. Jim has a dime, a nickel, and a quarter. How many different amounts of money can he form using one or more of these coins?

2. There are an equal number of red, blue, and green beads in a bag. One bead is picked, its color is noted and the bead is replaced. Then a second bead is picked.

a. Draw a tree diagram to show the outcomes.

b. What is the probability of picking two red beads?

c. What is the probability of picking one red and one green bead?

d. What is the probability of picking no red beads?

Angles

Practice 1   Angles on a Line

In each figure, $\overleftrightarrow{AC}$ is a line. Use a protractor to find the unknown angle measures.

1.

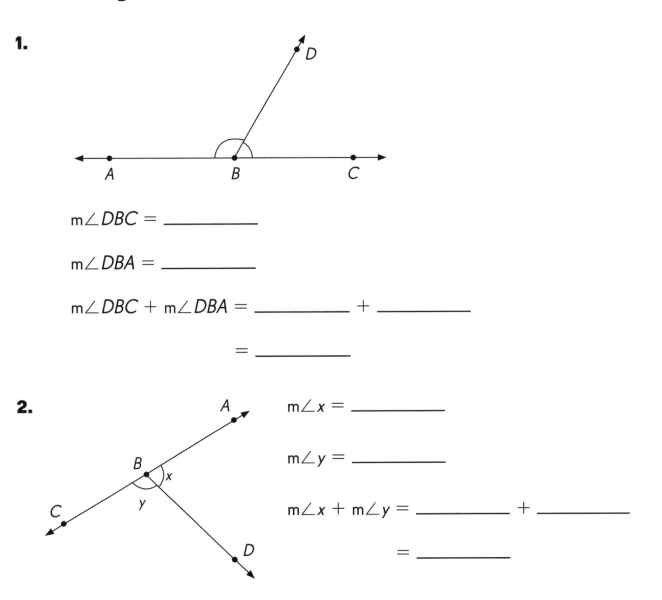

$m\angle DBC =$ _____

$m\angle DBA =$ _____

$m\angle DBC + m\angle DBA =$ _____ + _____

$=$ _____

2.

$m\angle x =$ _____

$m\angle y =$ _____

$m\angle x + m\angle y =$ _____ + _____

$=$ _____

$\overleftrightarrow{AC}$ **is a line. Use a protractor to find the unknown angle measures.**

3.

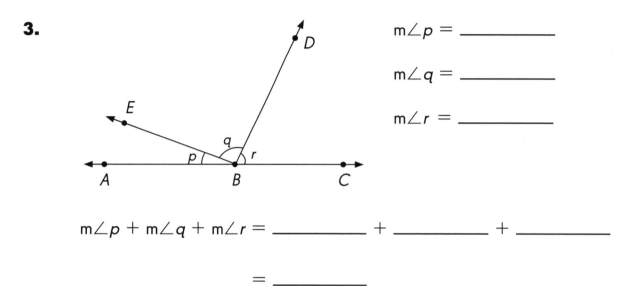

$m\angle p =$ _____

$m\angle q =$ _____

$m\angle r =$ _____

$m\angle p + m\angle q + m\angle r =$ _____ + _____ + _____

$=$ _____

Name the angles on each line.

4. $\overleftrightarrow{XZ}$ is a line.

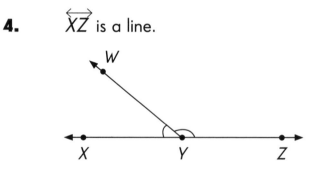

_____

5. $\overleftrightarrow{PR}$ is a line.

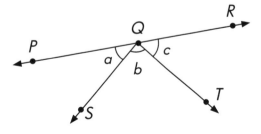

_____

Name each set of angles on a line.

6. $\overleftrightarrow{AC}$ is a line.

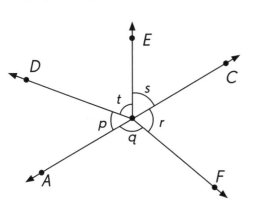

_____

_____

7. $\overleftrightarrow{AB}$ and $\overleftrightarrow{CD}$ are lines.

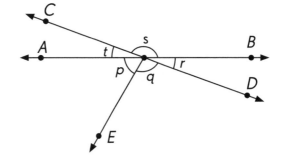

_____

_____

_____

Find the unknown angle measures.

8. $\overleftrightarrow{AC}$ is a line. Find the measure of $\angle DBC$.

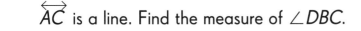
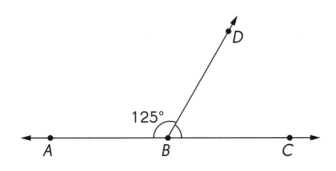

m$\angle DBC + 125° = 180°$

m$\angle DBC = 180° -$ _____

$=$ _____

9. $\overleftrightarrow{EG}$ is a line. Find the measure of $\angle HFE$.

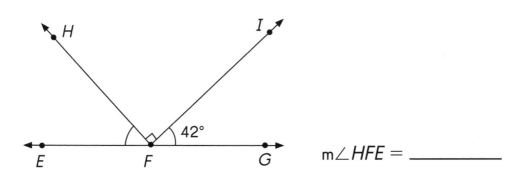

m$\angle HFE =$ _____

Find the unknown angle measures.

10. $\overleftrightarrow{OQ}$ is a line. Find the measure of $\angle SPT$.

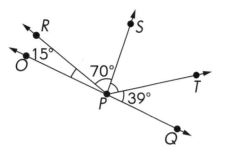

m$\angle SPT =$ _____

11. $\overleftrightarrow{AC}$ is a line. Find the measure of $\angle EBF$.

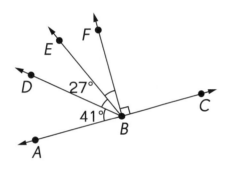

m$\angle EBF =$ _____

12. $\overleftrightarrow{JK}$ is a line. Find the measures of $\angle y$ and $\angle z$.

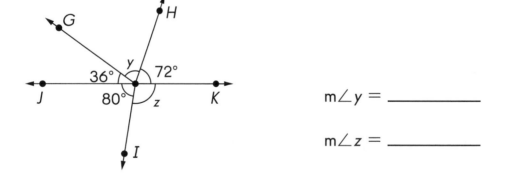

m$\angle y =$ _____

m$\angle z =$ _____

13. $\overleftrightarrow{EF}$ and $\overleftrightarrow{GH}$ are lines. Find the measures of $\angle a$ and $\angle b$.

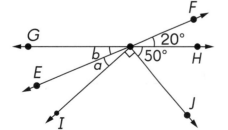

m$\angle a =$ _____

m$\angle b =$ _____

Practice 2 Angles at a Point

In each figure, the rays meet at a point. Use a protractor to find unknown angle measures.

1.

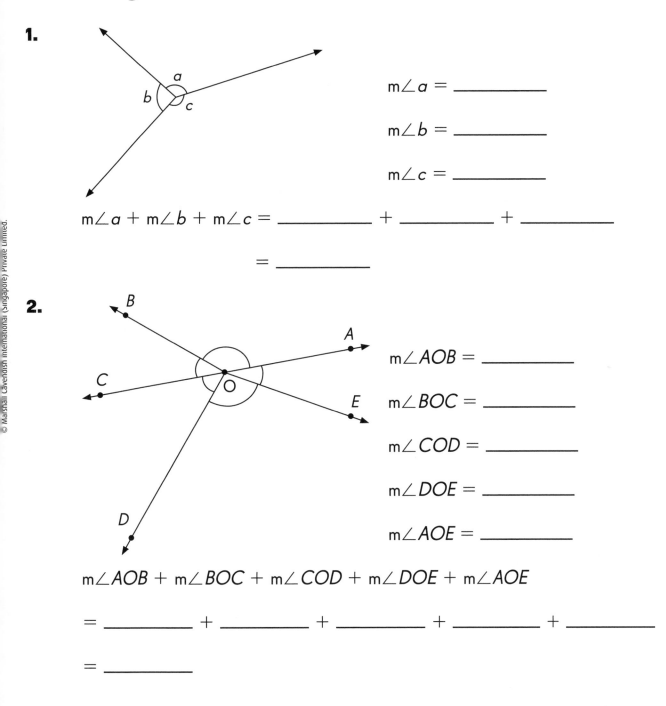

$m\angle a =$ _____

$m\angle b =$ _____

$m\angle c =$ _____

$m\angle a + m\angle b + m\angle c =$ _____ + _____ + _____

$=$ _____

2.

$m\angle AOB =$ _____

$m\angle BOC =$ _____

$m\angle COD =$ _____

$m\angle DOE =$ _____

$m\angle AOE =$ _____

$m\angle AOB + m\angle BOC + m\angle COD + m\angle DOE + m\angle AOE$

$=$ _____ + _____ + _____ + _____ + _____

$=$ _____

Name the angles at a point.

3.

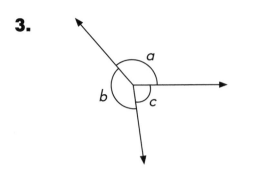

_____

4.

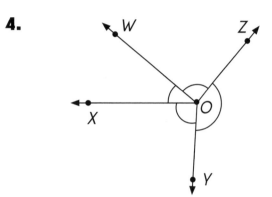

_____

5.

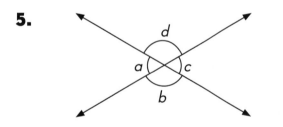

_____

6.

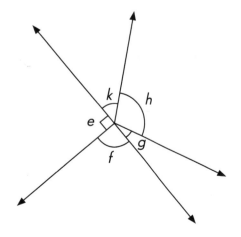

_____

Find the unknown angle measures.

7. Find the measure of ∠AOB.

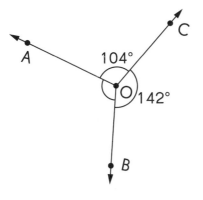

m∠AOB = _____

8. Find the measure of ∠a.

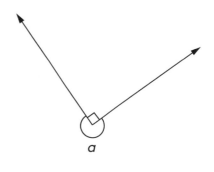

m∠a = _____

9. Find the measure of ∠b.

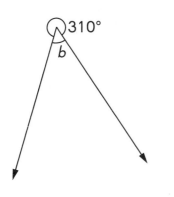

m∠b = _____

10. Find the measure of ∠c.

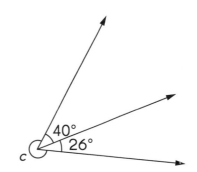

m∠c = _____

Find the unknown angle measures.

11. Find the measure of ∠q.

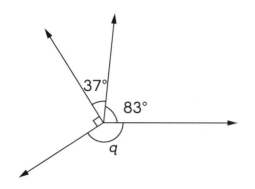

m∠q = _____

12. Find the measure of ∠r.

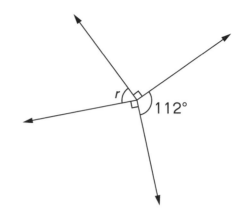

m∠r = _____

13. Find the measure of ∠a.

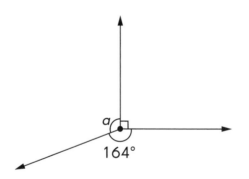

m∠a = _____

14. $\overleftrightarrow{PR}$ and $\overleftrightarrow{TU}$ meet at Q. Find the measures of ∠PQS and ∠TQR.

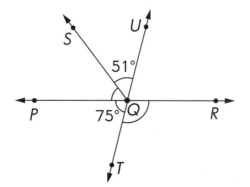

m∠PQS = _____

m∠TQR = _____

Practice 3   Vertical Angles

Complete.

1. $\overleftrightarrow{AB}$ and $\overleftrightarrow{CD}$ meet at O. Use a protractor to find unknown angle measures.

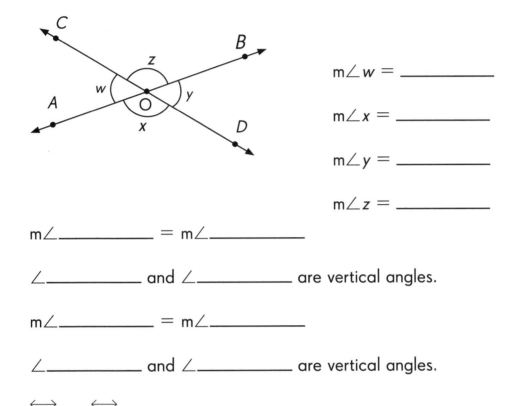

m∠w = _____

m∠x = _____

m∠y = _____

m∠z = _____

m∠_____ = m∠_____

∠_____ and ∠_____ are vertical angles.

m∠_____ = m∠_____

∠_____ and ∠_____ are vertical angles.

2. $\overleftrightarrow{XZ}$ and $\overleftrightarrow{VW}$ meet at Y. Use a protractor to find unknown angle measures.

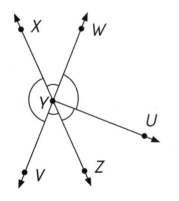

m∠XYW = _____

m∠WYU = _____

m∠UYZ = _____

m∠ZYV = _____

m∠VYX = _____

∠_____ and ∠_____ are vertical angles.

∠_____ and ∠_____ are vertical angles.

Complete.

3. Look at the star and its marked angles. In the table below, write three sets of:
   a. angles on a line,
   b. angles at a point,
   c. vertical angles.

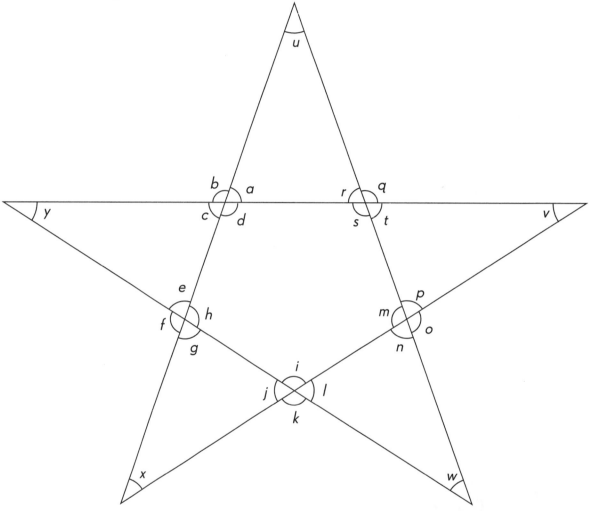

Angles on a Line	Angles at a Point	Vertical Angles
∠b and ∠c	∠a, ∠b, ∠c, and ∠d	∠a and ∠c

Draw.

4. Draw rays at *P* to form
  a. an angle whose measure forms a sum of 180° with the measure of ∠*x*,
  b. an angle whose measure is equal to the measure of ∠*x*.
  (Do not use a protractor to draw the angles.)

a.

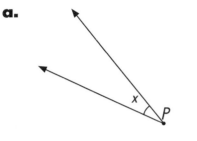

b.

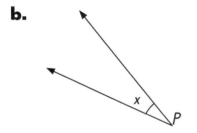

Find the unknown angle measures.

5. $\overleftrightarrow{AB}$ and $\overleftrightarrow{CD}$ meet at O. Find the measure of $\angle COB$.

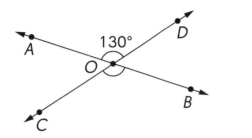

m$\angle COB =$ _____

6. $\overleftrightarrow{EF}$ and $\overleftrightarrow{GH}$ meet at O. Find the measures of $\angle GOF$ and $\angle EOH$.

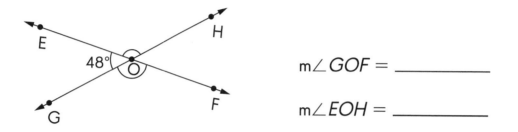

m$\angle GOF =$ _____

m$\angle EOH =$ _____

7. $\overleftrightarrow{RS}$ and $\overleftrightarrow{PQ}$ meet at N. Find the measures of $\angle PNR$, $\angle RNQ$, and $\angle QNS$.

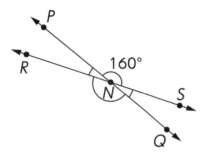

m$\angle PNR =$ _____

m$\angle RNQ =$ _____

m$\angle QNS =$ _____

Find the unknown angle measures.

8. $\overleftrightarrow{JK}$ and $\overleftrightarrow{LM}$ meet at O. Find the measure of $\angle NOK$.

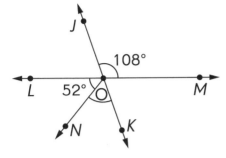

m$\angle NOK =$ _____

9. $\overleftrightarrow{AB}$, $\overleftrightarrow{CD}$, and $\overleftrightarrow{EF}$ meet at O. Find the measure of $\angle x$.

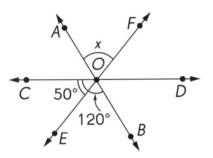

m$\angle x =$ _____

10. $\overleftrightarrow{AB}$ and $\overleftrightarrow{CD}$ meet at O. Find the measure of $\angle w$.

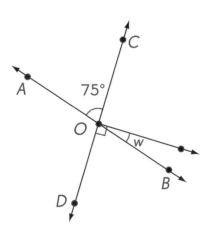

m$\angle w =$ _____

Find the unknown angle measures.

11. $\overleftrightarrow{QR}$ and $\overrightarrow{ST}$ meet at O. Find the measures of $\angle QOS$, $\angle TOR$, and $\angle SOR$.

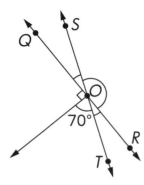

m$\angle QOS =$ _____

m$\angle TOR =$ _____

m$\angle SOR =$ _____

12. $\overleftrightarrow{AB}$ and $\overleftrightarrow{CD}$ meet at O. Find the measures of $\angle p$, $\angle q$, and $\angle r$.

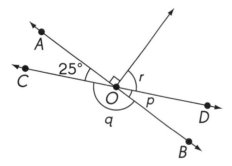

m$\angle p =$ _____

m$\angle q =$ _____

m$\angle r =$ _____

13. $\overleftrightarrow{UV}$, $\overleftrightarrow{WX}$, and $\overleftrightarrow{YZ}$ meet at O. Find the measure of $\angle UOW$.

m$\angle UOW$ = _____

14. $\overleftrightarrow{AB}$, $\overleftrightarrow{CD}$, and $\overleftrightarrow{EF}$ meet at O. Find the measures of $\angle x$ and $\angle y$.

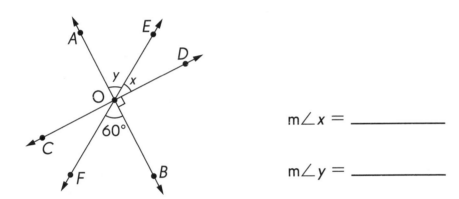

m$\angle x$ = _____

m$\angle y$ = _____

Math Journal

**Check the box for each correct statement.
Then explain your answer.**

1. $\overleftrightarrow{XY}$ is a line.

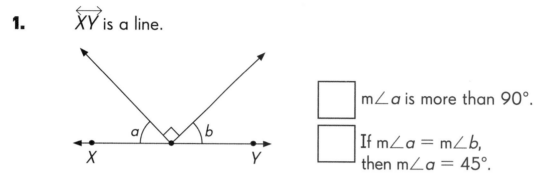

$\square$ $m\angle a$ is more than 90°.

$\square$ If $m\angle a = m\angle b$,
then $m\angle a = 45°$.

2. $\overleftrightarrow{AB}$ and $\overleftrightarrow{CD}$ meet at O.

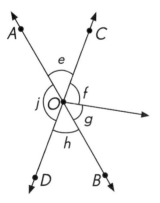

$\square$ $m\angle e = m\angle h$

$\square$ $m\angle f + m\angle g = m\angle j$

$\square$ $m\angle e = m\angle g$

Put On Your Thinking Cap!

Challenging Practice

Find the unknown angle measures. Explain.

1. $\overleftrightarrow{GJ}$ is a line. $\angle LHK$ is a right angle. Find the measure of $\angle LHJ$.

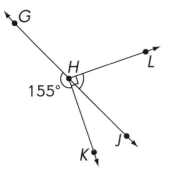

2. $\overleftrightarrow{MN}$ and $\overleftrightarrow{XY}$ meet at O and m$\angle a$ = m$\angle b$. Find the measure of $\angle c$.

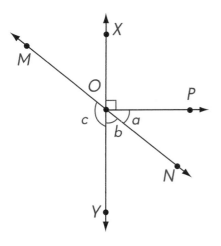

3. $\overleftrightarrow{AC}$ is a line. $\angle ABE$ and $\angle DBF$ are right angles.
Find the measure of $\angle FBC$.

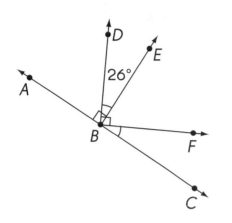

4. $\overleftrightarrow{AB}$ and $\overleftrightarrow{WX}$ meet at O. $\angle COB$ and $\angle YOX$ are right angles.
Find the measures of $\angle AOX$ and $\angle COY$.

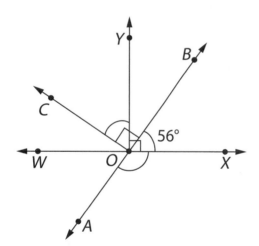

Put On Your Thinking Cap!

Problem Solving

Solve.

1. $\overleftrightarrow{JK}$ and $\overleftrightarrow{LM}$ are lines.
Check the box for each correct statement.

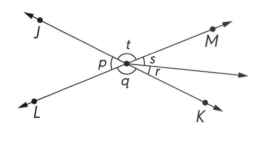

a. $m\angle p = m\angle r + m\angle s$ ☐

b. $m\angle s = m\angle p - m\angle r$ ☐

c. $m\angle q = 180° - m\angle p$ ☐

d. $m\angle r + m\angle s = m\angle p + m\angle q$ ☐

2. $\overleftrightarrow{AB}$, $\overleftrightarrow{CD}$, and $\overleftrightarrow{EF}$ meet at O. Find the sum of the measures of $\angle AOC$, $\angle FOD$, and $\angle BOE$.

$m\angle AOC + m\angle FOD + m\angle BOE =$ _____

3. $ABCD$ is a square. $\overrightarrow{BE}$ is a ray. Find the measure of $\angle x$.

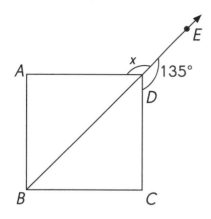

4. How many degrees does the hour hand of a clock turn between 3 P.M. and 7:30 P.M.?

5. $\overleftrightarrow{AB}$ is a line. The measures of $\angle a$ and $\angle b$ are whole numbers.

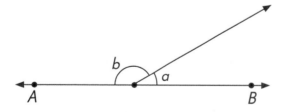

If the measure of $\angle b$ is twice that of $\angle a$, find the measures of $\angle a$ and $\angle b$.

Chapter 13 Properties of Triangles and Four-sided Figures

Practice 1 Classifying Triangles

Which of these triangles are equilateral, isosceles, or scalene? Use a centimeter ruler to find out.

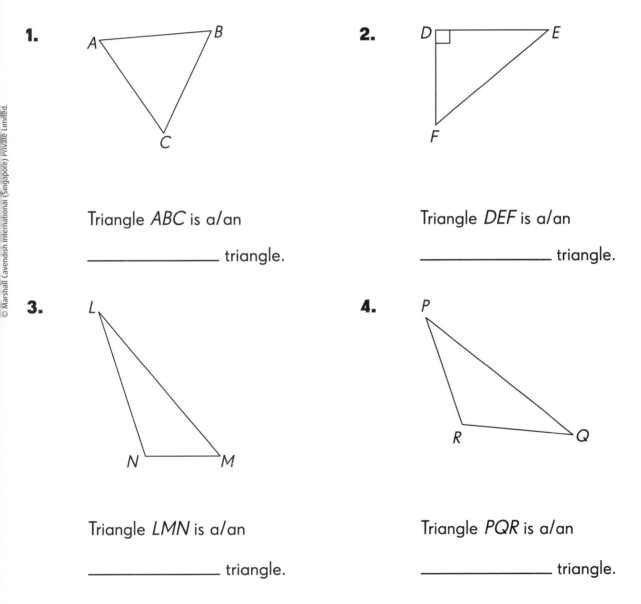

1.

Triangle *ABC* is a/an

_____ triangle.

2.

Triangle *DEF* is a/an

_____ triangle.

3.

Triangle *LMN* is a/an

_____ triangle.

4.

Triangle *PQR* is a/an

_____ triangle.

Which of these triangles are right, obtuse, or acute? Use a protractor to find out.

5.

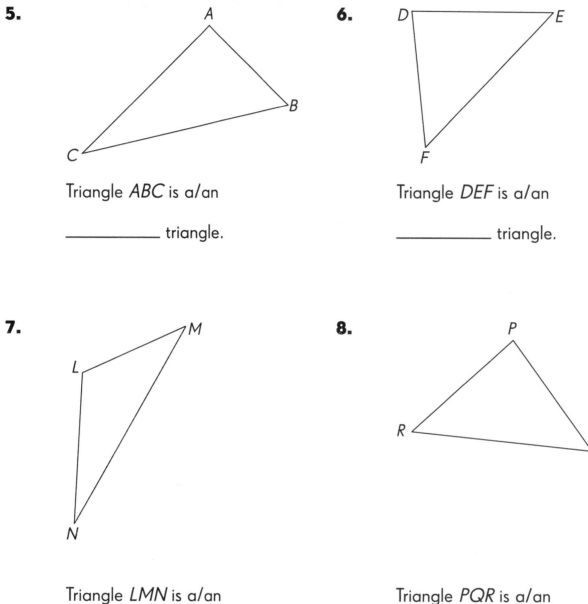

Triangle *ABC* is a/an

_____ triangle.

6.

Triangle *DEF* is a/an

_____ triangle.

7.

Triangle *LMN* is a/an

_____ triangle.

8.

Triangle *PQR* is a/an

_____ triangle.

Practice 2   Measures of Angles of a Triangle

Complete.

1.

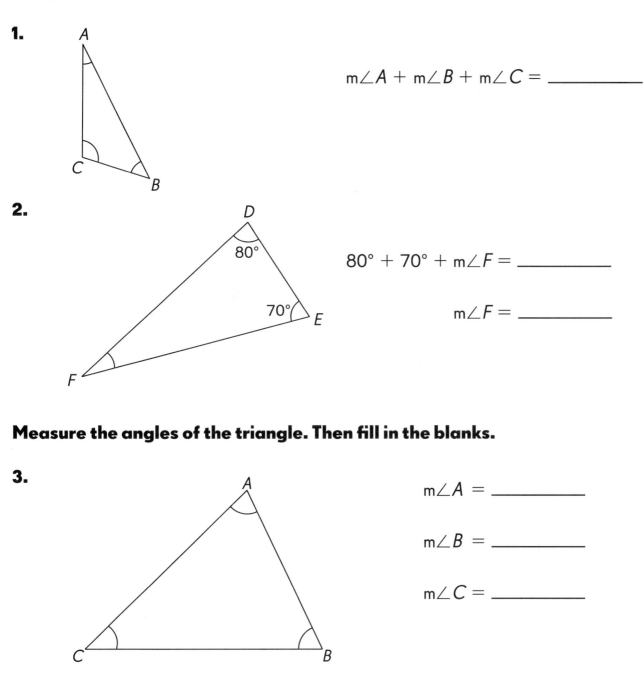

$m\angle A + m\angle B + m\angle C =$ _____

2.

$80° + 70° + m\angle F =$ _____

$m\angle F =$ _____

Measure the angles of the triangle. Then fill in the blanks.

3.

$m\angle A =$ _____

$m\angle B =$ _____

$m\angle C =$ _____

$m\angle A + m\angle B + m\angle C =$ _____ + _____ + _____

$=$ _____

The sum of the angle measures in the triangle is _____.

These triangles are not drawn to scale. Find the unknown angle measures.

4. Find the measure of ∠B.

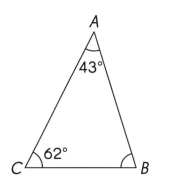

5. Find the measure of ∠D.

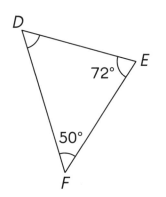

6. Find the measure of ∠H.

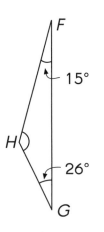

7. Find the measure of ∠QPS.

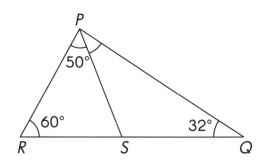

Practice 3   Right, Isosceles, and Equilateral Triangles

Complete. *ABC* and *EFG* are right triangles.

1.

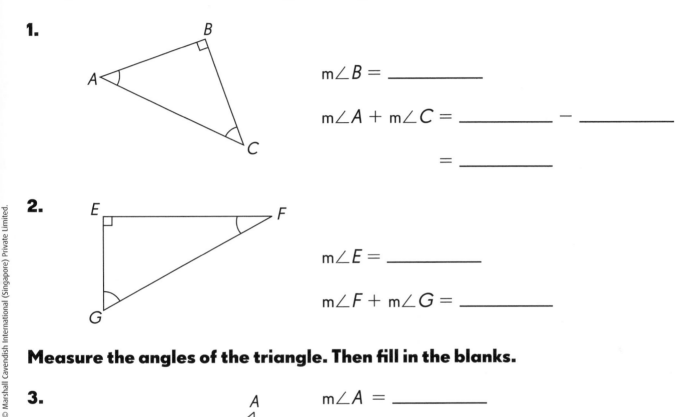

$m\angle B =$ _____

$m\angle A + m\angle C =$ _____ – _____

$=$ _____

2.

$m\angle E =$ _____

$m\angle F + m\angle G =$ _____

Measure the angles of the triangle. Then fill in the blanks.

3.

$m\angle A =$ _____

$m\angle B =$ _____

$m\angle C =$ _____

$m\angle A + m \angle C =$ _____

These triangles are not drawn to scale. Identify and shade the right triangles.

4.

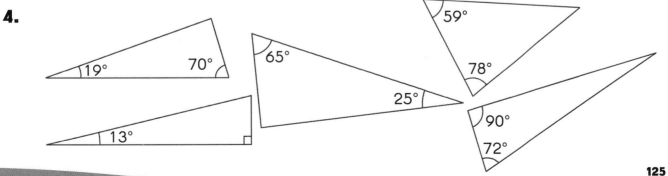

These triangles are not drawn to scale. Find the unknown angle measures.

5.   Find the sum of the measures of ∠A and ∠B.

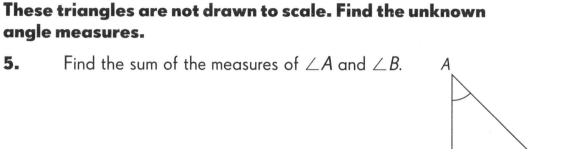

6.   Find the measure of ∠C.

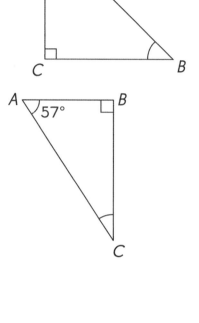

7.   Find the measures of ∠ADC and ∠ABC.

8.   Find the measures of ∠EGF and ∠DGE.

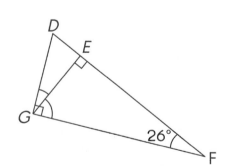

Name: _____   Date: _____

Complete. *XYZ* and *PQR* are isosceles triangles.

9.

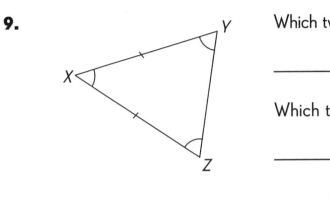

Which two sides are of equal length?

_____

Which two angles have equal measures?

_____

10.

Which two sides are of equal length?

_____

Which two angles have equal measures?

_____

These triangles are not drawn to scale. Identify and shade the isosceles triangles.

11.

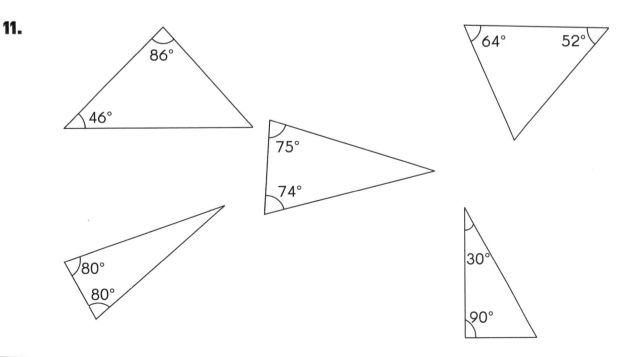

These triangles are not drawn to scale. Find the unknown angle measures.

12. Find the measure of ∠F.

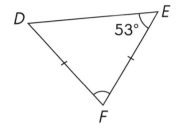

13. Find the measure of ∠C.

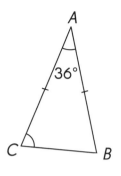

14. Find the measure of ∠TRS.

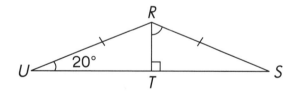

15. Find the measure of ∠d.

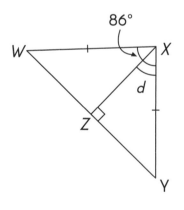

Name: _____   **Date:** _____

Complete. Use your protractor and centimeter ruler to measure the sides and angles. Which figure is an equilateral triangle? Check the box.

16.

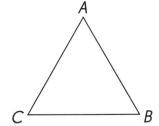

AB = _____ cm

BC = _____ cm

AC = _____ cm

m∠A = _____

m∠B = _____

m∠C = _____ ⬭

17.

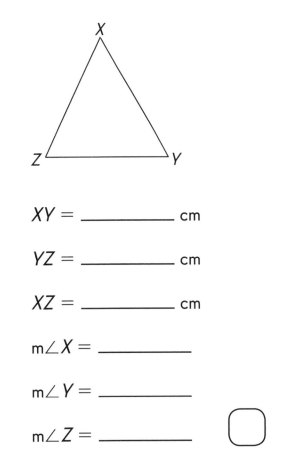

XY = _____ cm

YZ = _____ cm

XZ = _____ cm

m∠X = _____

m∠Y = _____

m∠Z = _____ ⬭

Complete. _ABC_ is an equilateral triangle.

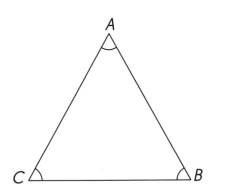

18. Which angles have measures equal to the measure of ∠A?

_____

19. Which sides have lengths equal to the length of $\overline{AB}$?

_____

20. What can you say about the angles of triangle _ABC_ ?

_____

These triangles are not drawn to scale. Identify and shade the equilateral triangles.

21.

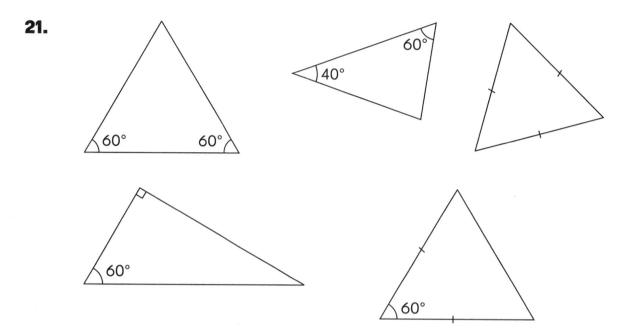

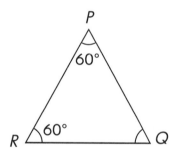

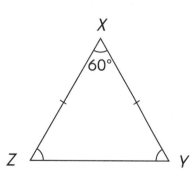

These triangles are not drawn to scale. Find the unknown angle measures.

22.   Find the measure of ∠Q.

```
        P
       /\
      /60°\
     /     \
    /       \
   /60°      \
  R‾‾‾‾‾‾‾‾‾‾Q
```

23.   Find the measures of ∠Y and ∠Z.

```
        X
       /\
      /60°\
     /     \
    /       \
   Z‾‾‾‾‾‾‾‾Y
```

Name: _____   Date: _____

These triangles are not drawn to scale. Find the unknown angle measures.

24. $WX = XY = YW$. Find the measure of $\angle d$.

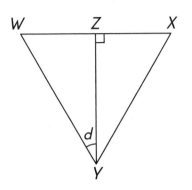

25.   Find the measure of $\angle e$.

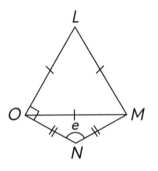

26.   Triangle PQR is an equilateral triangle. Triangle PST is an isosceles triangle. The measures of $\angle a$, $\angle b$, and $\angle c$ are the same. Find the measure of $\angle d$.

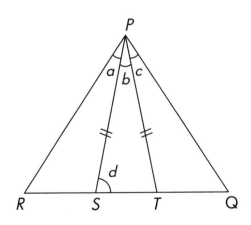

Math Journal

1. A teacher asked her students to sketch and label the angles of a triangle. These are the angle measures that three students chose to draw.

   Wayne: 120°, 80°, 10°   Ashley: 70°, 28°, 72°   Frank: 51°, 37°, 92°

   Will each student be able to draw his or her triangle? Explain your answer.

   Wayne: _____

   Ashley: _____

   Frank: _____

2. What are two ways to identify an isosceles triangle?

3. Jordan is measuring the angles of a triangle. He finds out that m∠A = m∠B = 60°. Without measuring ∠C, he says that triangle *ABC* is an equilateral triangle.

   Is he correct? Explain why.

   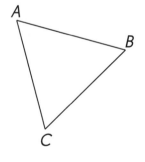

Practice 4   Triangle Inequalities

Complete. Measure the sides of the triangle to the nearest half inch. Then fill in the blanks.

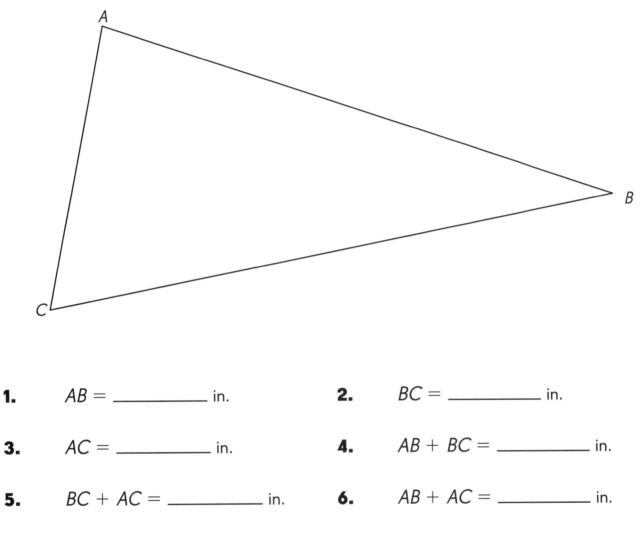

1. $AB =$ _____ in.   **2.** $BC =$ _____ in.

3. $AC =$ _____ in.   **4.** $AB + BC =$ _____ in.

5. $BC + AC =$ _____ in.   **6.** $AB + AC =$ _____ in.

Use your answers in Exercises 4 to 6. Fill in the blanks with *Yes* or *No*.

7.   Is $AB + BC > AC$? _____

8.   Is $BC + AC > AB$? _____

9.   Is $AB + AC > BC$? _____

Complete. Measure the sides of the triangle to the nearest centimeter. Then fill in the blanks.

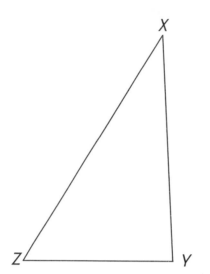

10. $XY =$ _____ cm

11. $YZ =$ _____ cm

12. $XZ =$ _____ cm

13. $XY + YZ =$ _____ cm

14. $YZ + XZ =$ _____ cm

15. $XY + XZ =$ _____ cm

Use your answers in Exercises 10 to 15. Write the sides of the triangle to make the inequalities true.

16. $XY + YZ >$ _____

17. $YZ + XZ >$ _____

18. $XY + XZ >$ _____

Show whether it is possible to form triangles with these lengths.

19.   6 in., 8 in., 12 in.

20.   9 in., 13 in., 3 in.

21.   2 cm, 4 cm, 7 cm

The lengths of two sides of each triangle are given. Name a possible length for the third side. The lengths are in whole centimeters or whole inches.

22.

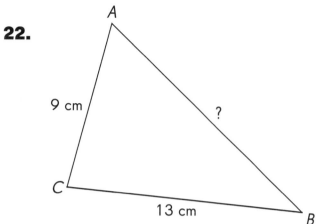

AB is greater than 10 centimeters.
A possible length for $\overline{AB}$ is

_____ centimeters.

23.

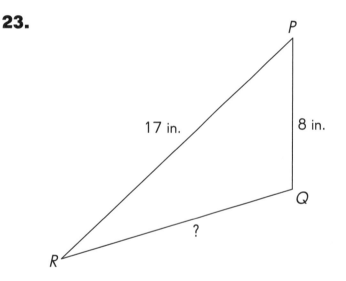

QR is greater than 9 inches.
A possible length for $\overline{QR}$ is

_____ inches.

Solve.

24. In the triangle *EFG*, *EF* = 21 centimeters, *FG* = 11 centimeters. The length of $\overline{EG}$ is in whole centimeters and is greater than 25 centimeters. What is a possible length of $\overline{EG}$?

Complete. Write the name of another side or angle of each rhombus.

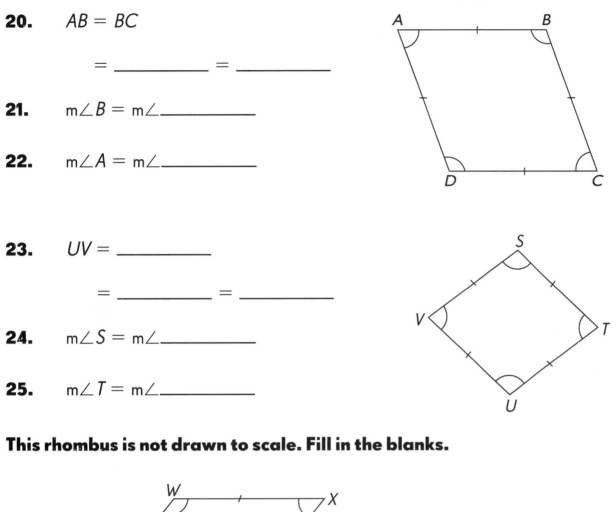

20. $AB = BC$

= _____ = _____

21. $m\angle B = m\angle$_____

22. $m\angle A = m\angle$_____

23. $UV =$ _____

= _____ = _____

24. $m\angle S = m\angle$_____

25. $m\angle T = m\angle$_____

This rhombus is not drawn to scale. Fill in the blanks.

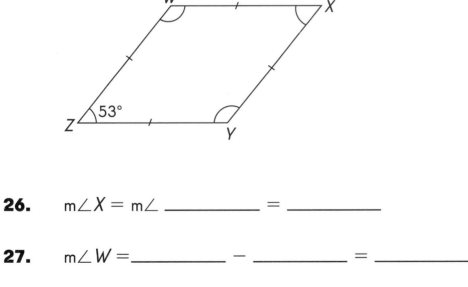

26. $m\angle X = m\angle$ _____ = _____

27. $m\angle W =$_____ − _____ = _____

28. $m\angle Y = m\angle$_____ = _____

**These rhombuses are not drawn to scale.
Find the unknown angle measures.**

29.

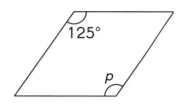

125°

p

30.

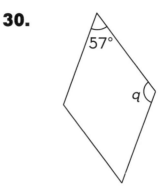

57°

q

31.

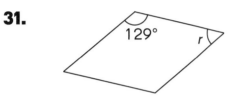

129°

r

32.

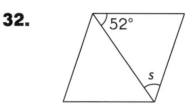

52°

s

33.

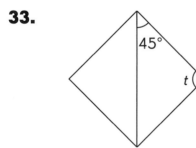

45°

t

34.

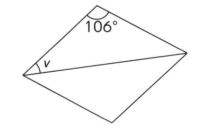

106°

v

Name: _____ **Date:** _____

Measure the unknown angles. Then fill in the blanks.

ABCD is a trapezoid where $\overline{AB} \parallel \overline{DC}$.

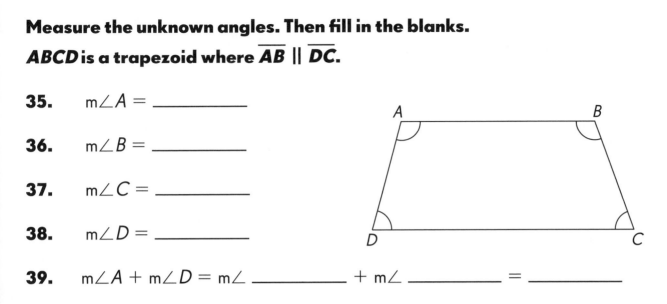

35. m∠A = _____

36. m∠B = _____

37. m∠C = _____

38. m∠D = _____

39. m∠A + m∠D = m∠ _____ + m∠ _____ = _____

These trapezoids are not drawn to scale.
Find the unknown angle measures.

40. $\overline{AB} \parallel \overline{DC}$

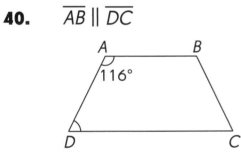

41. $\overline{EH} \parallel \overline{FG}$

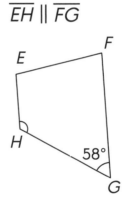

42. $\overline{JK} \parallel \overline{ML}$

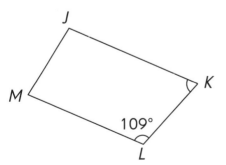

43. $\overline{PS} \parallel \overline{QR}$

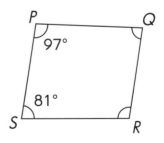

These trapezoids are not drawn to scale.
Find the unknown angle measures.

44. $\overline{TU} \parallel \overline{WV}$

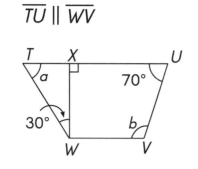

45. $\overline{VW} \parallel \overline{YX}$

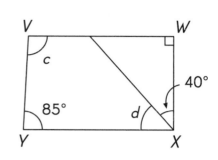

46. $\overline{AB} \parallel \overline{DC}$

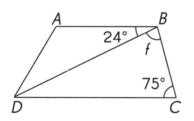

47. $\overline{EH} \parallel \overline{FG}$

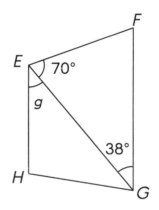

Put On Your Thinking Cap!

Challenging Practice

This figure is a rhombus and $\angle ADO = \angle CDO$. Find the measure of $\angle DOC$.

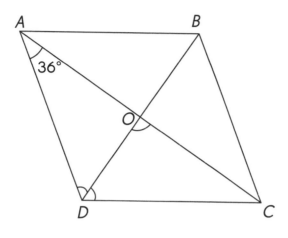

Put On Your Thinking Cap!

Problem Solving

1. *ABCD* is a trapezoid in which $\overline{AD} \parallel \overline{BC}$. Find the measure of $\angle CED$.

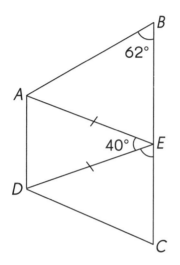

2. *ABCD* is a parallelogram and *CDEF* is a rhombus. Find the measure of $\angle ADE$.

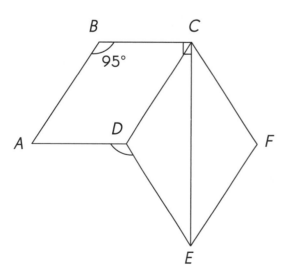

for Chapters 11 to 13

Concepts and Skills

The double bar graph shows the number of pairs of black jeans and blue jeans produced in a factory in three days.

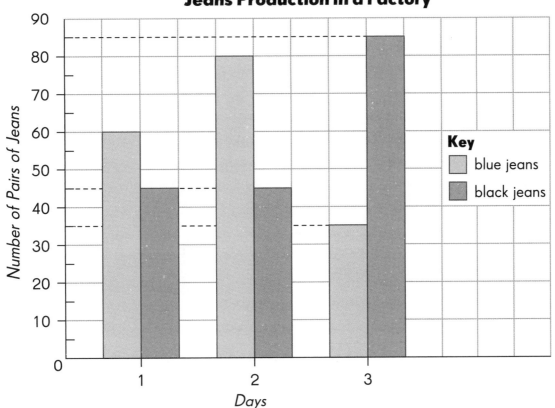

Jeans Production in a Factory

Complete. Use the data in the graph on page 145. *(Lesson 11.1)*

1. On day 2, _____ more pairs of blue jeans than black jeans are produced.

2. On day _____ and day _____ , the same number of pairs of black jeans are produced.

3. The greatest number of blue jeans is produced on day _____.

4. On day 1, the difference between the number of pairs of blue jeans and black jeans produced is _____.

5. The total number of pairs of jeans produced in the three days is _____.

6. The ratio of the number of pairs of black jeans produced to the number of pairs of blue jeans produced on day 3 is _____.

7. Express the number of black jeans produced on day 1 as a fraction of the number of blue jeans produced on day 1. _____

8. Express the total number of blue jeans produced as a percent of the total number of jeans produced in the three days. _____

© Marshall Cavendish International (Singapore) Private Limited.

Complete the graph using the data in the table.
Then answer the questions. *(Lesson 11.2)*

Amount of Milk (Quarts)	1	2	3	4
Number of Cups of Milk	4	8	12	16

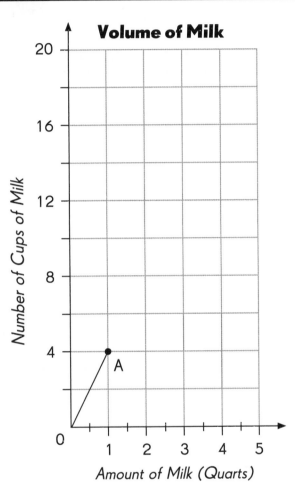

Volume of Milk

Number of Cups of Milk (vertical axis)

Amount of Milk (Quarts) (horizontal axis)

9.　What are the coordinates of point *A*? _____

10.　How many quarts of milk are in 12 cups? _____

11.　How many cups of milk are in $3\frac{1}{2}$ quarts of milk? _____

12.　How many cups of milk are in 5 quarts of milk? _____

Make an organized list to find the number of combinations. *(Lesson 11.3)*

Barry's Yogurt Shop sells frozen yogurt with a topping. A customer can pick one of three flavors: vanilla, strawberry, and blueberry. The customer can pick one of three toppings: nuts, raisins, and sprinkles.

13. List all the possible combinations of yogurt flavor and topping.

Yogurt Flavor	Topping

14. There are _____ combinations.

Find the number of combinations. *(Lesson 11.3)*

Brenda has 1 red, 1 green and 1 gold bracelet. She has 4 pairs of earrings: stud, hoop, button, and dangling. She wants to find all the combinations of 1 bracelet and 1 pair of earrings that she can wear.

15. Draw a tree diagram to show the possible combinations.

16. Find the number of combinations by multiplication.

_____ × _____ = _____

There are _____ combinations.

Complete. *(Lesson 11.4)*

A bag has 5 green toothbrushes and 7 yellow toothbrushes. Tim and Cathy each pick a toothbrush, and then return it to the bag. They do this for 20 times each. The table shows some of their results.

17. Complete the table.

	Number of Times a Green Toothbrush is Picked	Number of Times a Yellow Toothbrush is Picked	Probability of Picking a Green Toothbrush	Probability of Picking a Yellow Toothbrush
Tim	12			
Cathy		9		

18. The theoretical probability of picking a yellow toothbrush is _____.

19. The experimental probability of picking a green toothbrush that Tim's results

show is _____.

Find the unknown angle measures. *(Lesson 12.1)*

20. $\overleftrightarrow{AB}$ is a line.

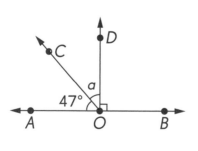

m∠a = _____

21. $\overleftrightarrow{AB}$ is a line. The measures of ∠a, ∠b, and ∠c are equal.

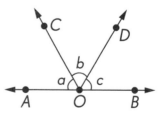

m∠a = m∠b = m∠c

= _____

Find the unknown angle measures. *(Lessons 12.1 and 12.2)*

22. $\overleftrightarrow{AB}$ is a line.

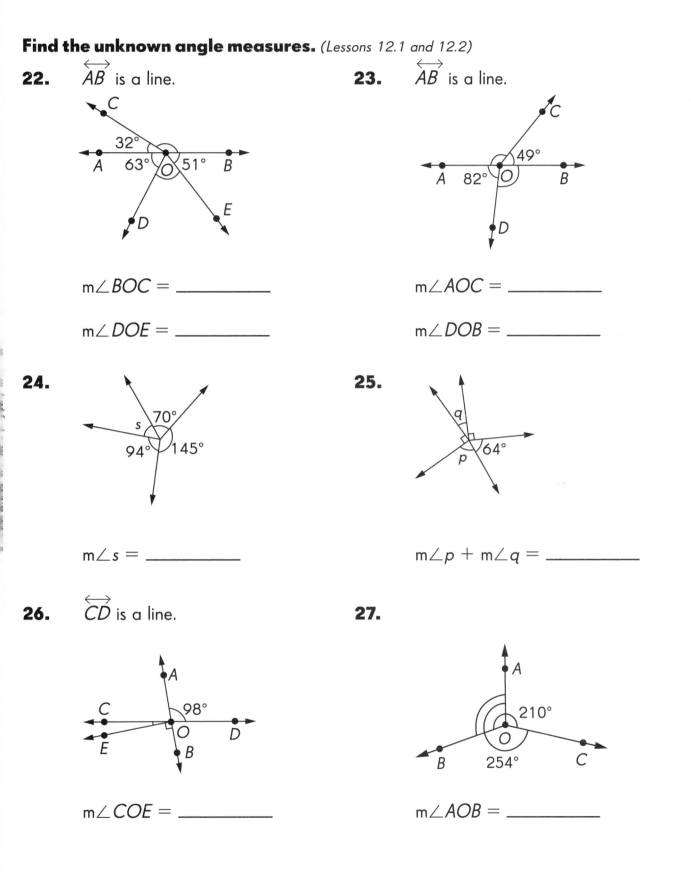

m∠BOC = _____

m∠DOE = _____

23. $\overleftrightarrow{AB}$ is a line.

m∠AOC = _____

m∠DOB = _____

24.

m∠s = _____

25.

m∠p + m∠q = _____

26. $\overleftrightarrow{CD}$ is a line.

m∠COE = _____

27.

m∠AOB = _____

Find the unknown angle measures. (Lesson 12.3)

$\overleftrightarrow{AB}$, $\overleftrightarrow{CD}$, and $\overleftrightarrow{EF}$ are lines.

28.

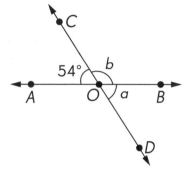

m∠a = _____

m∠b = _____

29.

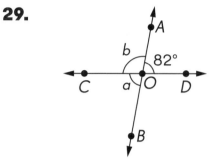

m∠a = _____

m∠b = _____

30.

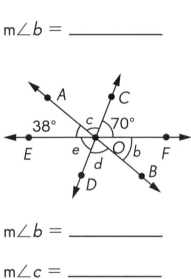

m∠b = _____

m∠c = _____

m∠d = _____

m∠e = _____

m∠b + m∠d + m∠e

= _____

31.

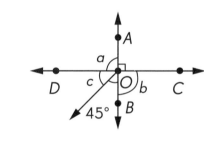

m∠a = _____

m∠b = _____

m∠c = _____

Find the unknown angle measures. Then classify triangle *ABC* as an acute, obtuse, or right triangle. *(Lessons 13.1 to 13.3)*

32.

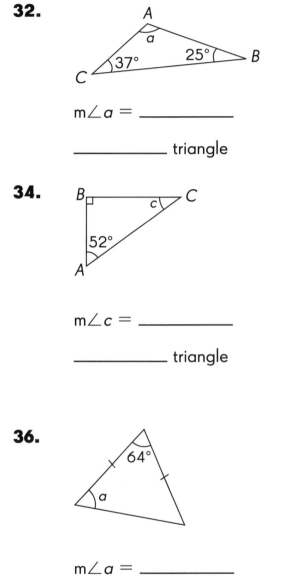

m∠a = _____

_____ triangle

33.

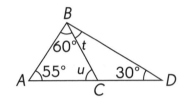

m∠b = _____

_____ triangle

34.

m∠c = _____

_____ triangle

35.

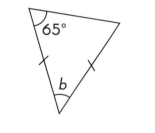

m∠u = _____

m∠t = _____

_____ triangle

36.

m∠a = _____

37.

m∠b = _____

38.   *AB = BC = AD*

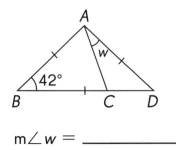

m∠w = _____

39.

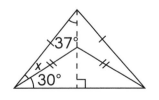

m∠x = _____

Find the unknown angle measures. *(Lesson 13.3)*

40.

41. $ZY = YX = XZ$

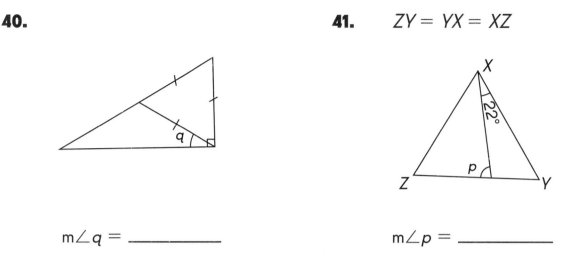

$m\angle q =$ _____ $m\angle p =$ _____

Measure the sides of the triangles in inches. Then fill in the blanks.
(Lessons 13.1 and 13.4)

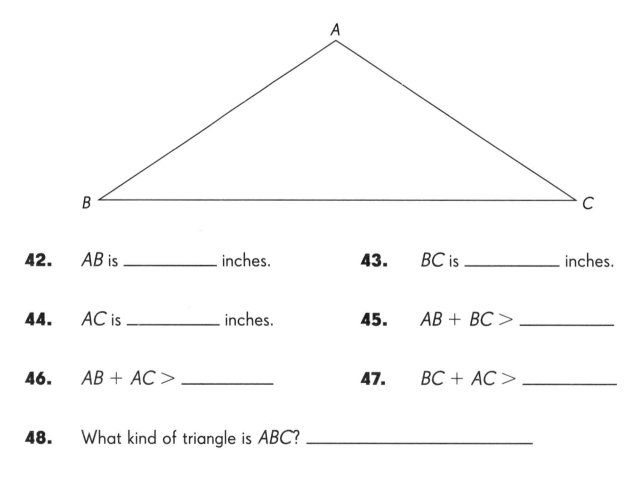

42. AB is _____ inches.   **43.** BC is _____ inches.

44. AC is _____ inches.   **45.** $AB + BC >$ _____

46. $AB + AC >$ _____   **47.** $BC + AC >$ _____

48. What kind of triangle is ABC? _____

Find the unknown angle measures in each parallelogram. *(Lesson 13.5)*

49.

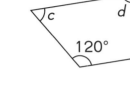

m∠c = _____

m∠d = _____

m∠e = _____

50.

m∠f = _____

Find the unknown angle measures in each rhombus. *(Lesson 13.5)*

51.

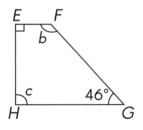

m∠b = _____

m∠c = _____

52.

m∠d = _____

m∠e = _____

Find the unknown angle measures in each trapezoid. *(Lesson 13.5)*

53. In *EFGH*, $\overline{EF} \parallel \overline{HG}$.

m∠b = _____

m∠c = _____

54. In *PQRS*, $\overline{PS} \parallel \overline{QR}$.

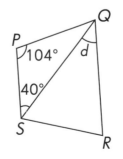

m∠d = _____

Problem Solving

Solve. Show your work.

The graph shows a measurement in yards (*x*-axis) and its corresponding measurement in feet (*y*-axis).

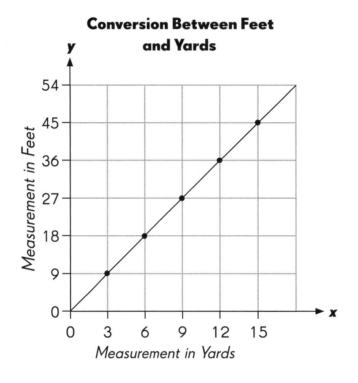

Conversion Between Feet and Yards

55. The cost of 3 yards of fabric is $24. What is the cost of 36 feet of fabric?

Solve. Show your work.

56. Each letter of the word JOURNAL is written on separate cards and put into a bag. First, one card is drawn. Then, the card is colored blue or yellow.

   a. Draw a tree diagram to show the possible combinations of cards and colors.

   b. What is the theoretical probability of picking a combination with a vowel?

Solve. Show your work.

57. In the triangle ABC, $AB = 4$ centimeters, $BC = 7$ centimeters and AC is longer than 8 centimeters. If the length of $\overline{AC}$ is in whole centimeters, what are the possible lengths of $\overline{AC}$?

58. $ABCD$ is a trapezoid and $ABED$ is a parallelogram. $\overline{AB} \parallel \overline{DC}$, $\overline{AD} \parallel \overline{BE}$, and $BE = BC$. Find the measure of $\angle BCE$.

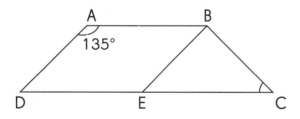

Chapter 14

Three-Dimensional Shapes

Practice 1   Prisms and Pyramids

Identify the type of prism and the shapes of the faces.

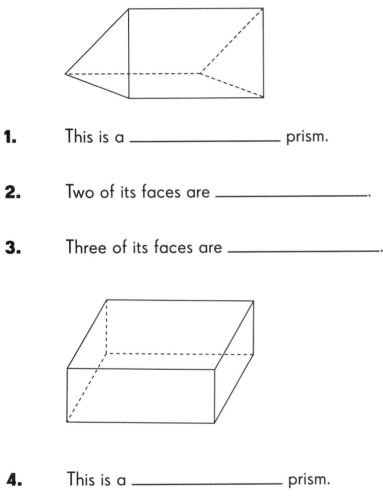

1.   This is a _____ prism.

2.   Two of its faces are _____.

3.   Three of its faces are _____.

4.   This is a _____ prism.

5.   All its faces are _____.

Complete the table.

Type of Prism	Number of Faces	Number of Edges	Number of Vertices
6.			
7.			
8.			

Identify the type of pyramid and the shape of the faces.

9.   This is a _____ pyramid.

10.   All its faces are _____.

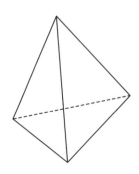

Identify the type of pyramid and the shapes of the faces.

11. This is a _____ pyramid.

12. One of its faces is a _____.

13. Four of its faces are _____.

Complete the table.

Type of Pyramid	Number of Faces	Number of Edges	Number of Vertices
14.			
15.			

Name the solid formed by each net.

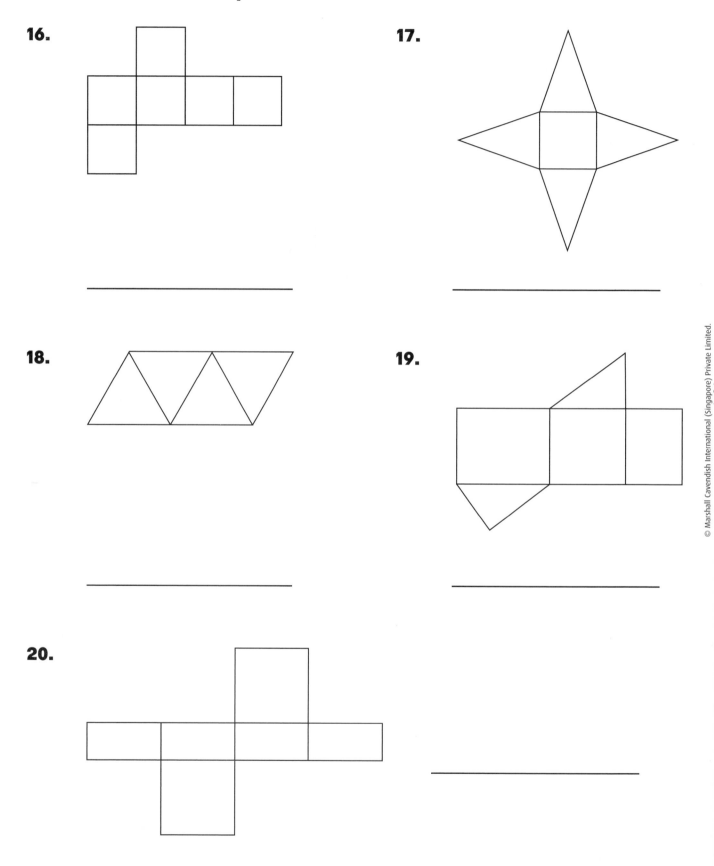

16.

_____

17.

_____

18.

_____

19.

_____

20.

_____

Name: _____   Date: _____

Practice 2   Cylinder, Sphere, and Cone

Identify each solid shape.

1.

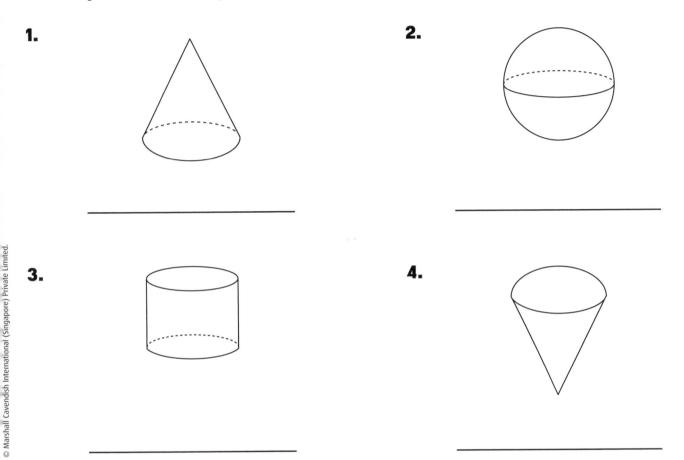

_____

2.

_____

3.

_____

4.

_____

Identify the shape of the base of each solid shape.

5.

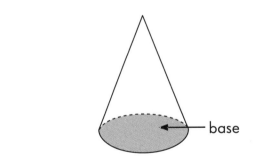

base

_____

6.

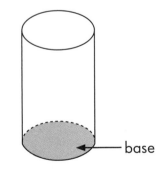

base

_____

Describe the labeled surface of each solid shape.

7.

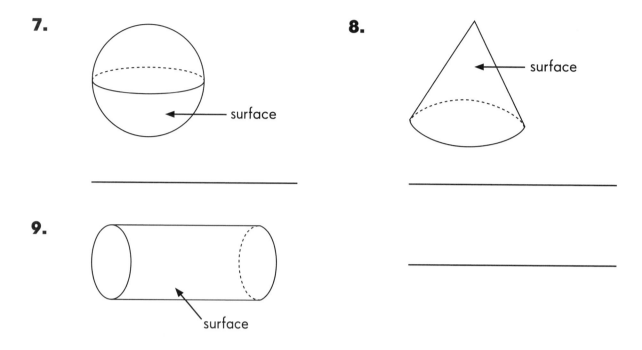

surface

_____

8.

surface

_____

9.

surface

_____

Complete.

10. The height of a cylinder is 4 centimeters. Complete the net of this open cylinder.

Put On Your Thinking Cap!

Challenging Practice

Find the number of cubes in each prism.

1.

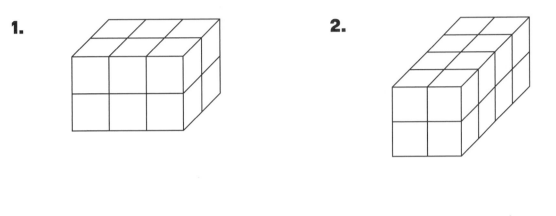

_____ cubes

2.

_____ cubes

Each solid is cut vertically along the line shown. Identify the solid shapes that result.

3.

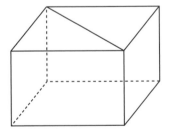

_____

4.

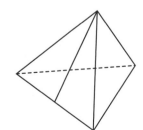

_____

Put On Your Thinking Cap!

Problem Solving

You may trace, cut out, and fold the nets.

Which of these are nets of a cube? Check the boxes.

1.

2.

3.

4.

5.

6.

7.

8.

Chapter 15 Surface Area and Volume

Practice 1   Building Solids Using Unit Cubes

Find the number of unit cubes used to build each solid.

1.

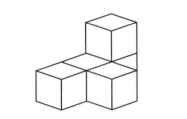

_____ unit cubes

2.

_____ unit cubes

3.

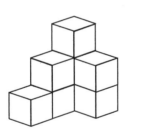

_____ unit cubes

4.

_____ unit cubes

5.

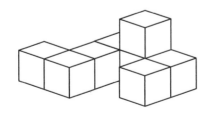

_____ unit cubes

6.

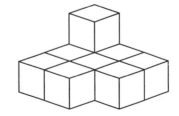

_____ unit cubes

Find the number of unit cubes used to build each solid.

7.

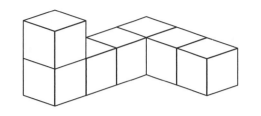

_____ unit cubes

8.

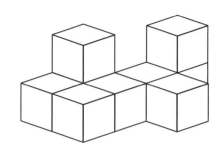

_____ unit cubes

9.

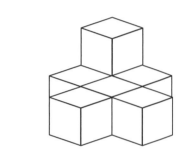

_____ unit cubes

10.

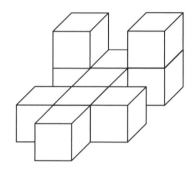

_____ unit cubes

11.

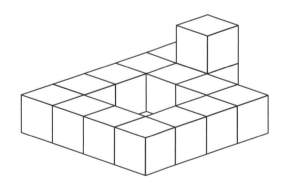

_____ unit cubes

Practice 2   Drawing Cubes and Rectangular Prisms

Draw on dot paper.

1.   Draw a unit cube.

2.   Draw two different views of a rectangular prism made up of 2 unit cubes.

3.   Draw two different solids made up of 3 unit cubes each.

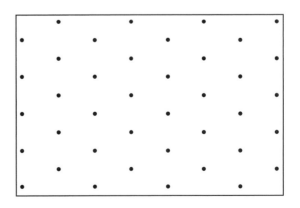

Draw each cube or rectangular prism on the dot paper.

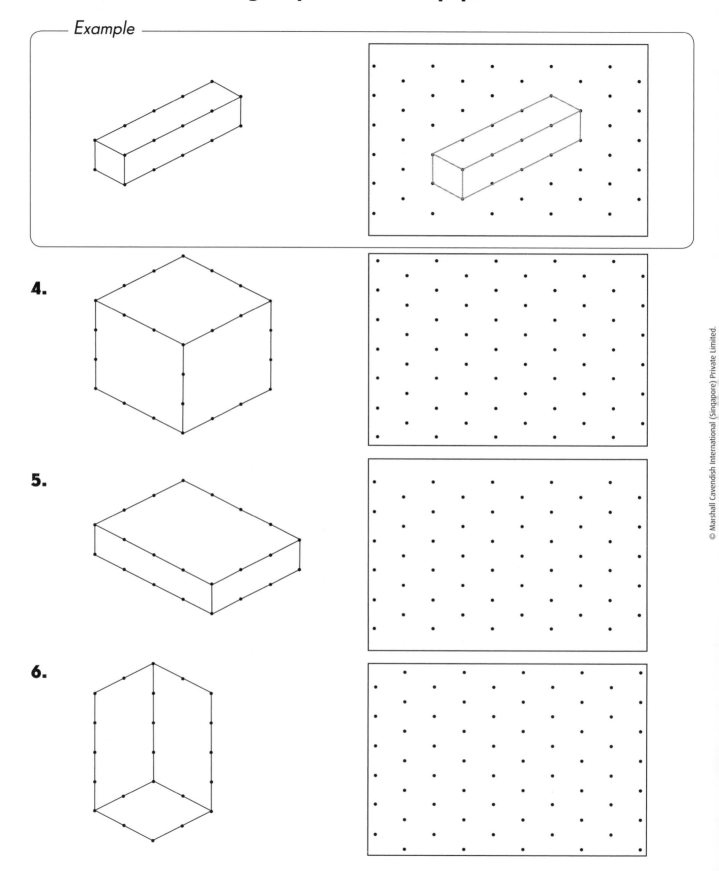

Example

4.

5.

6.

Draw each cube or rectangular prism on the dot paper.

7.

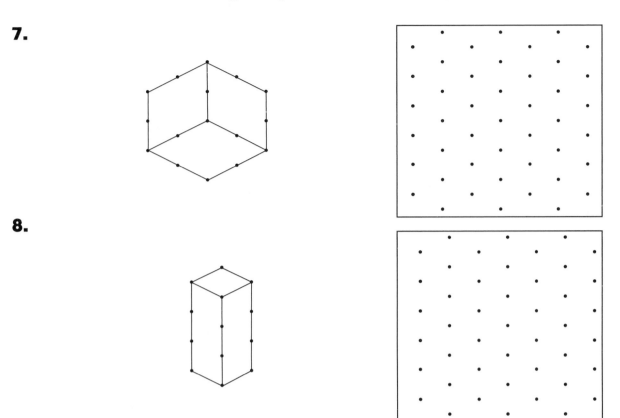

8.

Draw a cube with edges 4 times as long as the edges of this unit cube.

9.

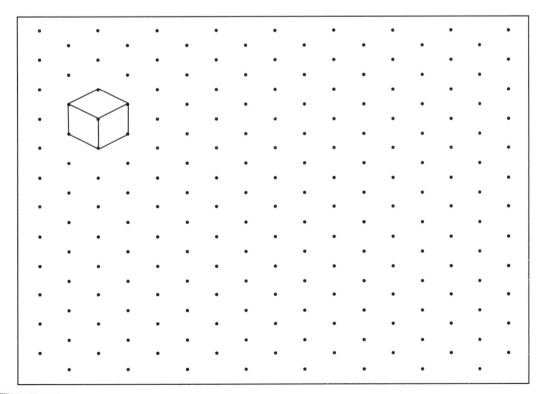

Complete the drawing of each cube or rectangular prism.

10.

11.

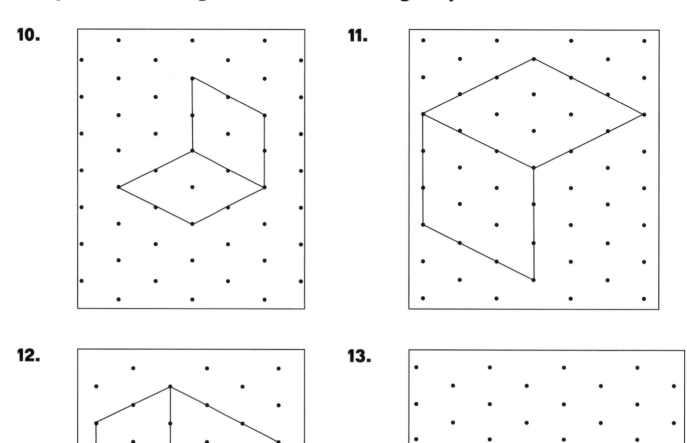

12.

13.

Practice 3   Nets and Surface Area

Find the surface area of each cube.

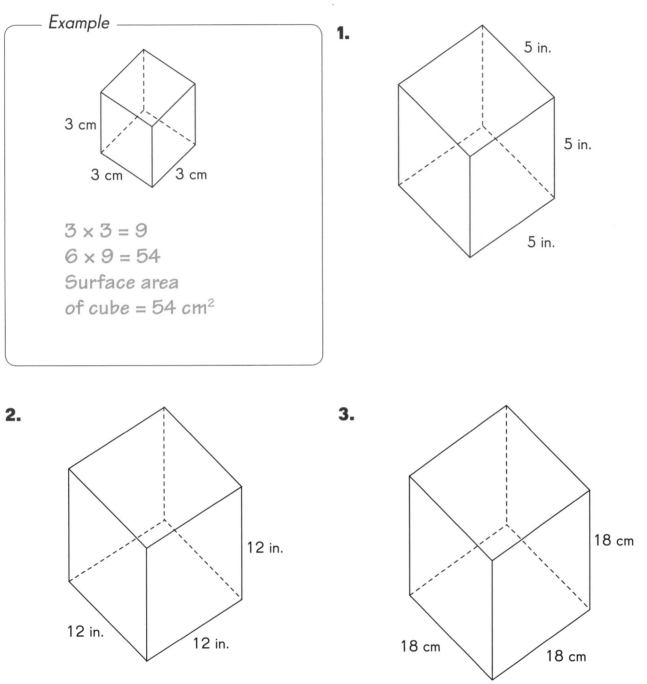

Example

3 cm
3 cm   3 cm

$3 \times 3 = 9$
$6 \times 9 = 54$
Surface area
of cube = 54 cm²

1.

5 in.
5 in.
5 in.

2.

12 in.
12 in.   12 in.

3.

18 cm
18 cm   18 cm

Find the surface area of each rectangular prism.

Example

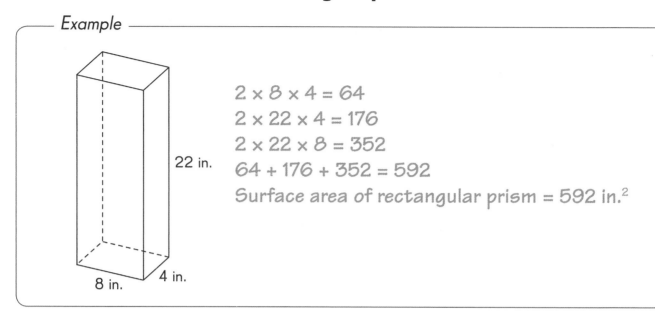

$2 \times 8 \times 4 = 64$
$2 \times 22 \times 4 = 176$
$2 \times 22 \times 8 = 352$
$64 + 176 + 352 = 592$
Surface area of rectangular prism = 592 in.^{2}

4.

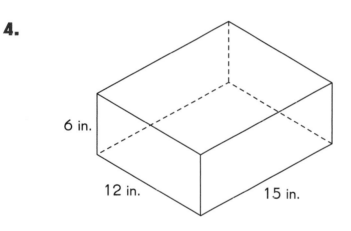

5.

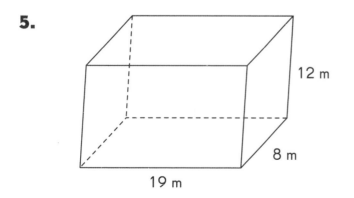

Find the surface area of each triangular prism.

Example

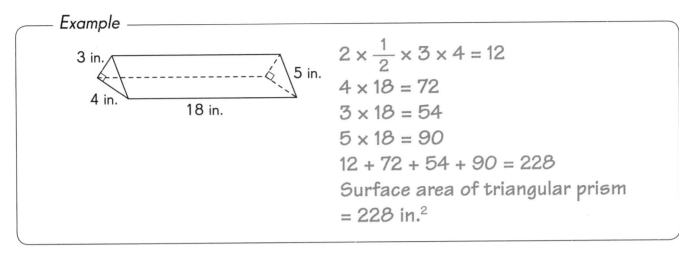

$2 \times \dfrac{1}{2} \times 3 \times 4 = 12$

$4 \times 18 = 72$

$3 \times 18 = 54$

$5 \times 18 = 90$

$12 + 72 + 54 + 90 = 228$

Surface area of triangular prism

$= 228 \text{ in.}^2$

6.

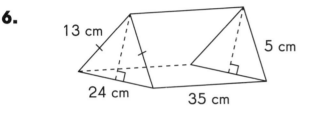

Solve. Show your work.

7. Jeffrey cuts out the net of a box he wants to make.
Find the surface area of the box.

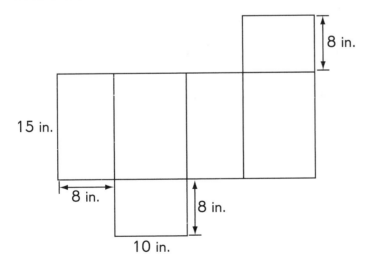

Solve. Show your work.

8. This glass fish tank does not have a cover. Find the total area of the glass panels used to make the tank.

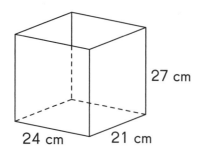

27 cm

24 cm   21 cm

9. The tank shown is made of steel. It does not have a cover. Find the area of steel sheet used to make the tank.

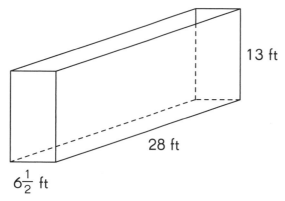

13 ft

28 ft

$6\frac{1}{2}$ ft

10. A rectangular piece of poster board measures 60 centimeters by 80 centimeters. Linn draws the net of a box on the poster board and cuts it out. If the box measures 10 centimeters by 16 centimeters by 27 centimeters, what is the area of the poster board left?

Practice 4 Understanding and Measuring Volume

These solids are formed by stacking unit cubes in the corner of a room. Find the volume of each solid.

1.

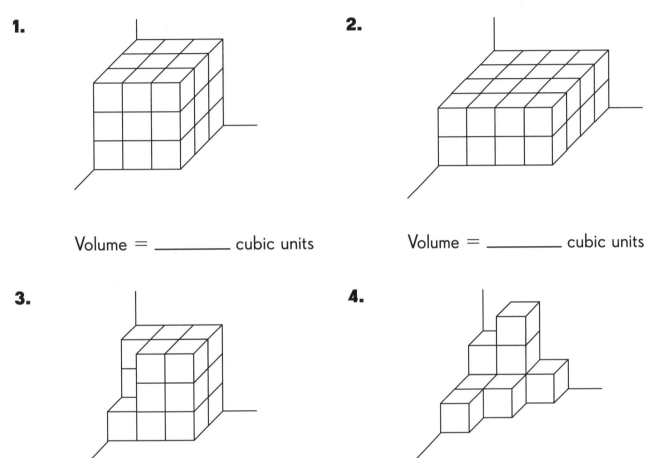

Volume = _____ cubic units

2.

Volume = _____ cubic units

3.

Volume = _____ cubic units

4.

Volume = _____ cubic units

These solids are formed by stacking 1-centimeter cubes in the corner of a room. Find the volume of each solid.

5.

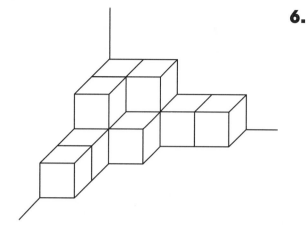

Volume = _____ cm³

6.

Volume = _____ cm³

7.

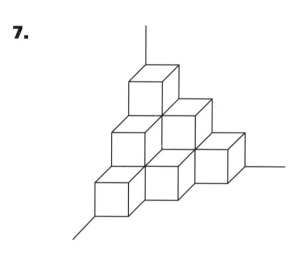

Volume = _____ cm³

8.

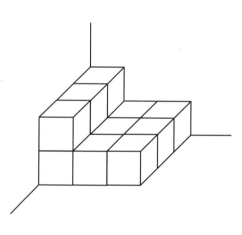

Volume = _____ cm³

9.

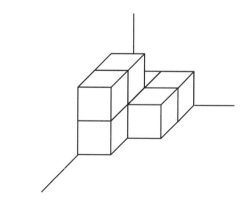

Volume = _____ cm³

10.

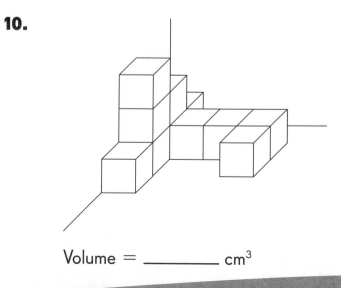

Volume = _____ cm³

Name: _____   **Date:** _____

These solids are built using 1-centimeter cubes.
Find the volume of each solid. Then compare their volumes
and fill in the blanks.

11.

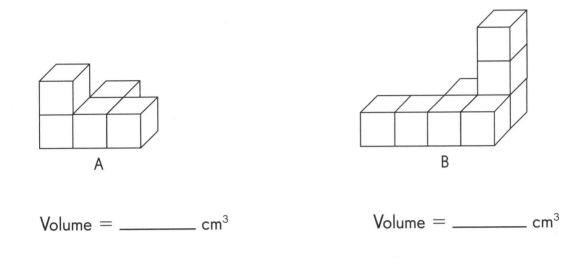

A   B

Volume = _____ cm³   Volume = _____ cm³

Solid _____ has a greater volume than solid _____.

These solids are built using 1-meter cubes.
Find the volume of each solid. Then compare their volumes
and fill in the blanks.

12.

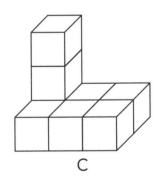   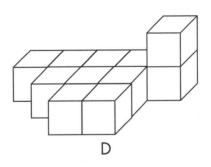

C   D

Volume = _____ m³   Volume = _____ m³

Solid _____ has a lesser volume than solid _____.

These solids are built using 1-inch cubes. Find the volume of each solid. Then compare their volumes and fill in the blanks.

13.

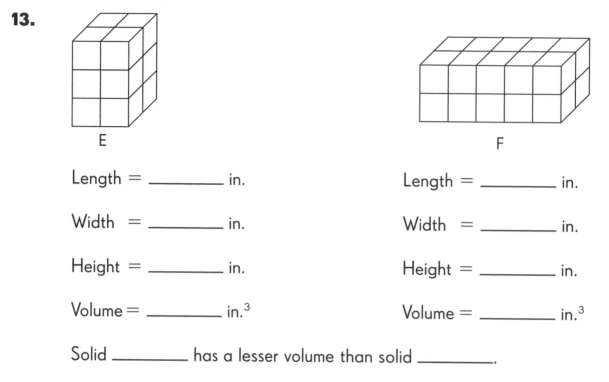

E

F

Length = _____ in.

Width = _____ in.

Height = _____ in.

Volume = _____ in.³

Length = _____ in.

Width = _____ in.

Height = _____ in.

Volume = _____ in.³

Solid _____ has a lesser volume than solid _____.

These solids are built using 1-foot cubes. Find the volume of each solid. Then compare their volumes and fill in the blanks.

14.

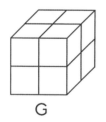

G

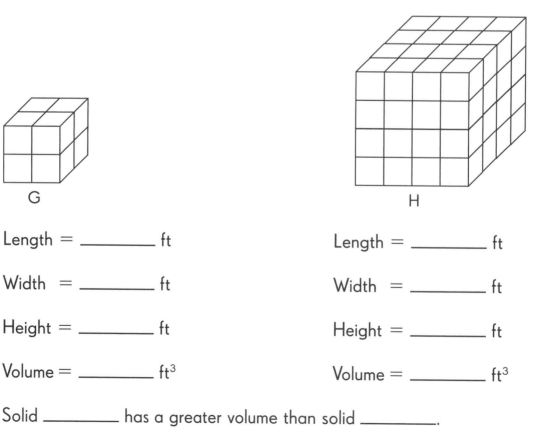

H

Length = _____ ft

Width = _____ ft

Height = _____ ft

Volume = _____ ft³

Length = _____ ft

Width = _____ ft

Height = _____ ft

Volume = _____ ft³

Solid _____ has a greater volume than solid _____.

Practice 5 Volume of a Rectangular Prism and Liquid

Write the length, width, and height of each rectangular prism or cube.

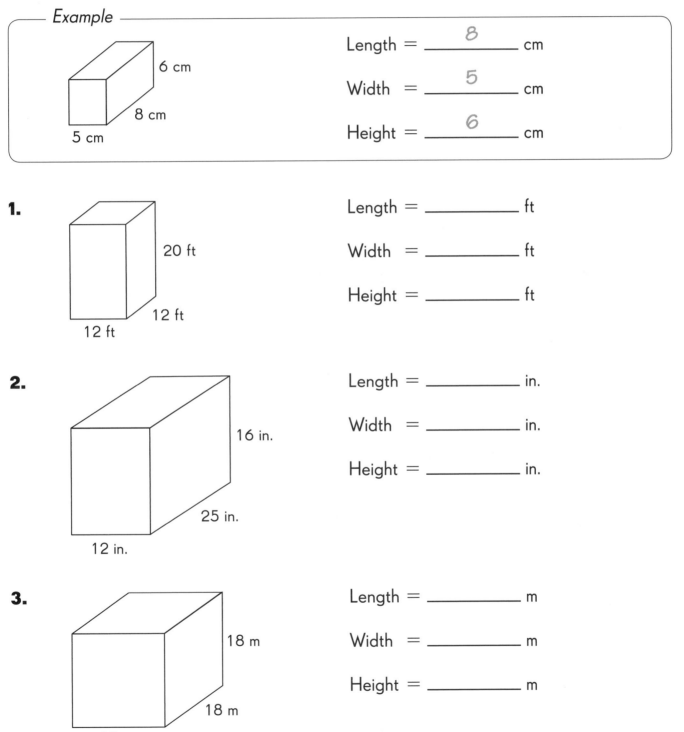

Example

6 cm
8 cm
5 cm

Length = _____8_____ cm

Width = _____5_____ cm

Height = _____6_____ cm

1.

20 ft
12 ft
12 ft

Length = _____ ft

Width = _____ ft

Height = _____ ft

2.

16 in.
25 in.
12 in.

Length = _____ in.

Width = _____ in.

Height = _____ in.

3.

18 m
18 m
18 m

Length = _____ m

Width = _____ m

Height = _____ m

Find the volume of each rectangular prism.

4.

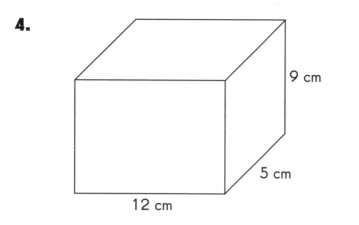

The length of the rectangular prism is _____ centimeters.

The width of the rectangular prism is _____ centimeters.

The height of the rectangular prism is _____ centimeters.

Volume of the rectangular prism = length × width × height

$$= \underline{\hspace{1.5cm}} \times \underline{\hspace{1.5cm}} \times \underline{\hspace{1.5cm}}$$

$$= \underline{\hspace{1.5cm}} \text{ cm}^3$$

5.

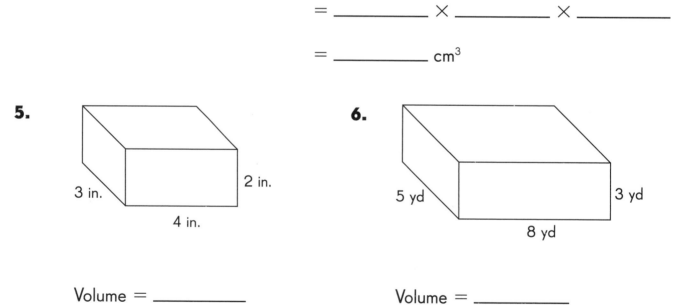

Volume = _____

6.

Volume = _____

Find the volume of each rectangular prism or cube.

7.

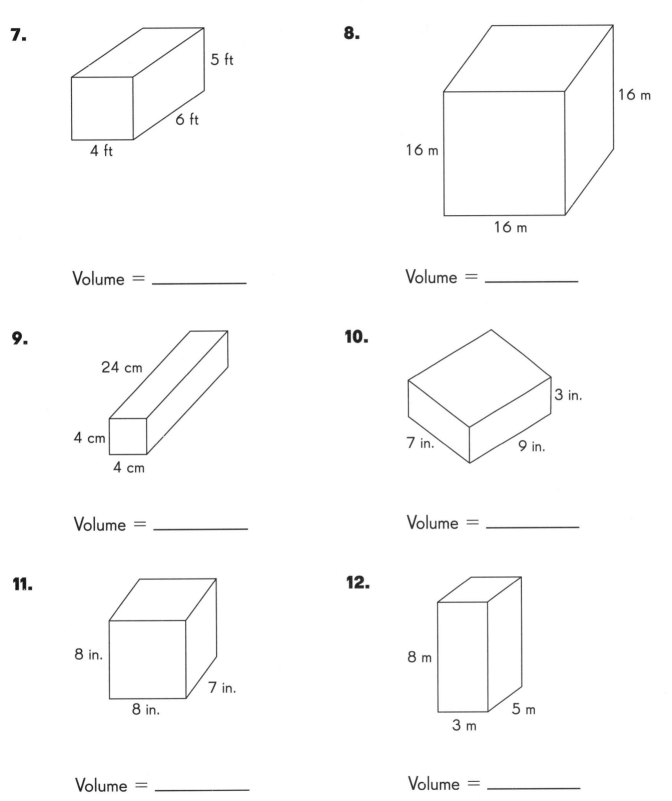

5 ft

6 ft

4 ft

Volume = _____

8.

16 m

16 m

16 m

Volume = _____

9.

24 cm

4 cm

4 cm

Volume = _____

10.

3 in.

7 in.

9 in.

Volume = _____

11.

8 in.

7 in.

8 in.

Volume = _____

12.

8 m

5 m

3 m

Volume = _____

Find the volume of each rectangular prism.

	Length	Width	Height	Volume
13.	5 cm	12 cm	9 cm	
14.	10 in.	25 in.	14 in.	
15.	7 m	12 m	8 m	
16.	24 ft	10 ft	15 ft	

Solve. Show your work.

17. Find the volume of a cube with edges measuring 9 centimeters.

18. A rectangular prism has a length of 8 feet and a height of 5 feet. Its length is twice its width. Find the volume of the rectangular prism.

19. The base of a rectangular prism is a square whose sides each measure 9 inches. The height of the rectangular prism is 11 inches. Find its volume.

Name: _____ **Date:** _____

Practice 6   Volume of a Rectangular Prism and Liquid

Write each measure in milliliters.

1. 690 cm³ = _____

2. 207 cm³ = _____

3. 2,000 cm³ = _____

4. 4,600 cm³ = _____

Write each measure in cubic centimeters.

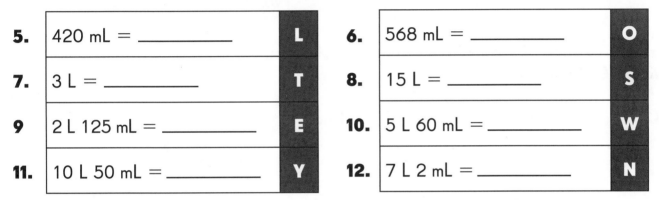

5. 420 mL = _____ **L**

7. 3 L = _____ **T**

9 2 L 125 mL = _____ **E**

11. 10 L 50 mL = _____ **Y**

6. 568 mL = _____ **O**

8. 15 L = _____ **S**

10. 5 L 60 mL = _____ **W**

12. 7 L 2 mL = _____ **N**

Do you know which national park is the oldest in the United States? Match the letters to the answers to find out.

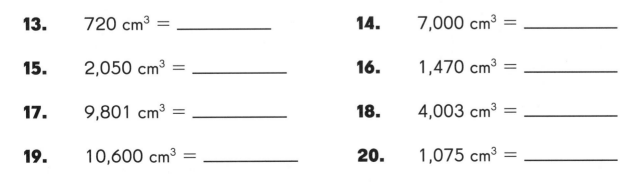

10,050 2,125   420   420   568   5,060 15,000 3,000   568   7,002 2,125

National Park

Write each measure in liters and milliliters.

13. 720 cm³ = _____

14. 7,000 cm³ = _____

15. 2,050 cm³ = _____

16. 1,470 cm³ = _____

17. 9,801 cm³ = _____

18. 4,003 cm³ = _____

19. 10,600 cm³ = _____

20. 1,075 cm³ = _____

Find the volume of water in each rectangular tank in milliliters.
(Hint: 1 cm³ = 1 mL)

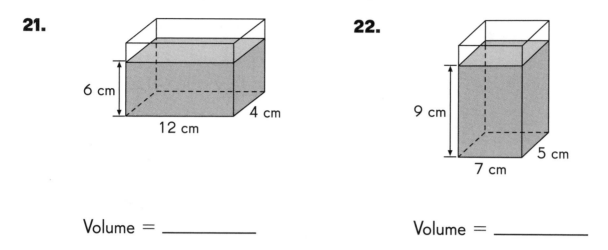

21.

6 cm

12 cm   4 cm

Volume = _____

22.

9 cm

7 cm   5 cm

Volume = _____

Find the volume of water in each rectangular tank in liters and milliliters.
(Hint: 1,000 cm³ = 1 L)

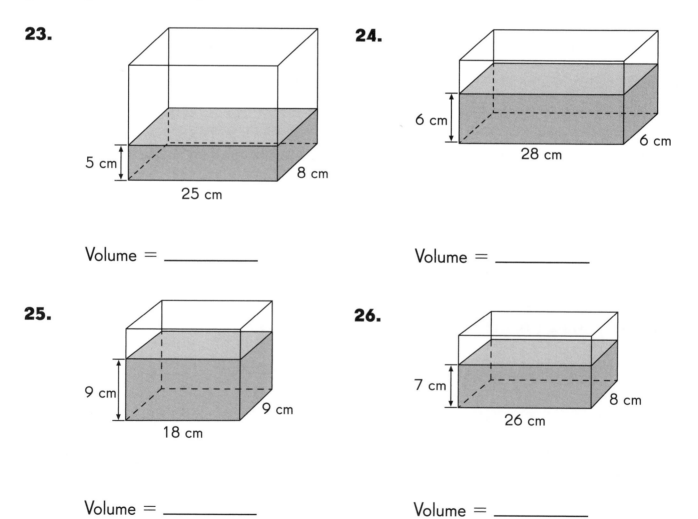

23.

5 cm

25 cm   8 cm

Volume = _____

24.

6 cm

28 cm   6 cm

Volume = _____

25.

9 cm

18 cm   9 cm

Volume = _____

26.

7 cm

26 cm   8 cm

Volume = _____

Name: _____ **Date:** _____

Solve. Show your work.

31. This container is half-filled with oil. What is the volume of oil
in the container? Give your answer in liters and milliliters.

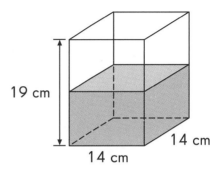

32. A cubical tank whose edges each measure 12 centimeters is half-filled
with water. The water is poured into an empty rectangular tank measuring
10 centimeters by 8 centimeters by 7 centimeters until it is full.
How much water is left in the cubical tank? Give your answer in milliliters.

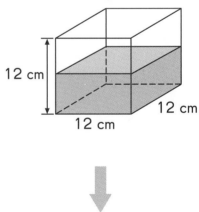

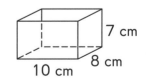

Solve. Show your work.

33. The rectangular swimming pool shown contains 600 cubic meters of water. How much more water has to be added so that the water level is 1 meter from the top?

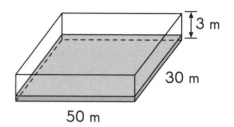

34. The rectangular tank shown is filled completely with water. How much water must be taken out so the height of the water level in the tank is 10 centimeters? Give your answer in milliliters.

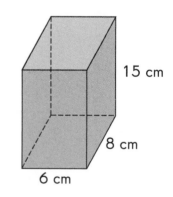

Solve. Show your work.

35. The large rectangular tank shown is $\frac{4}{5}$-filled with water.
The water is then poured into the smaller rectangular container
until it is full. How much water is left in the tank? Give your answer
in liters and milliliters.

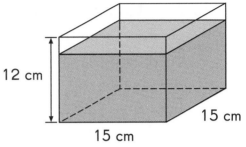

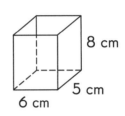

36. Water flows into this tank at 8 liters per minute.
How long will it take to fill the tank?

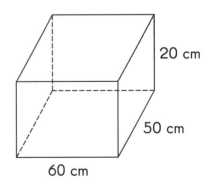

 Math Journal

This rectangular container is $\frac{2}{5}$-filled with water. How much more water is needed to increase the height of the water level to 3 centimeters?

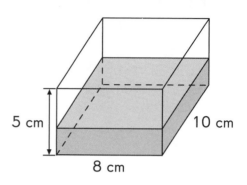

5 cm

10 cm

8 cm

Show two methods of solving this problem. Which method do you prefer? Why?

Put On Your Thinking Cap!

Challenging Practice

1. A rectangular tank is half-filled with water. Another 650 cubic centimeters of water are needed to make it $\frac{3}{5}$ full. How much water will be in the tank when it is $\frac{3}{5}$ full?

2. A cube has a surface area of 216 square centimeters.
   A second cube has edges that are 3 times as long. How much greater is the surface area of the second cube than the first cube?

 Put On Your Thinking Cap!

Problem Solving

A prism has a square base whose edges each measure 5 centimeters. The ratio of its height to its width is 4 : 1. Find the volume of the rectangular prism in cubic centimeters.

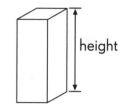

height

for Chapters 14 and 15

Concepts and Skills

Name each solid. Then write the number of faces and vertices, and the shapes of the faces. (Lesson 14.1)

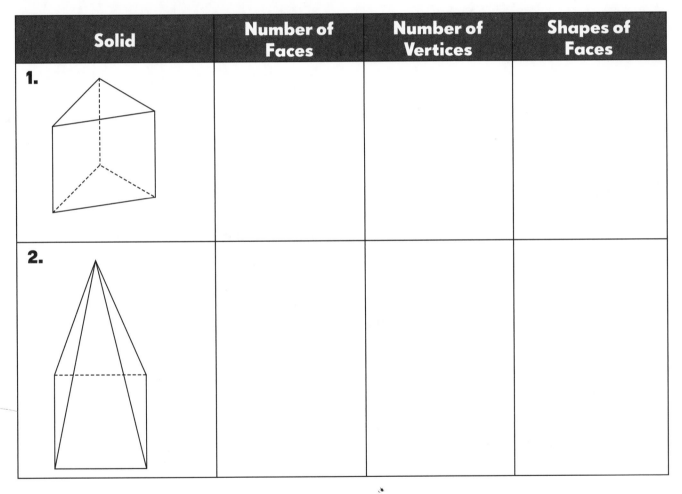

Solid	Number of Faces	Number of Vertices	Shapes of Faces
1.			
2.			

Name the solid formed from each net. *(Lesson 14.1)*

3.

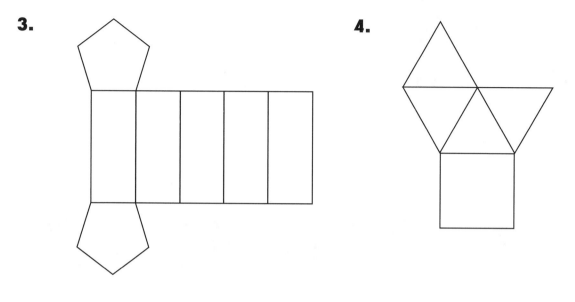

_____

4.

_____

Complete. *(Lesson 14.2)*

5. A _____ has two parallel and congruent bases that are joined by a curved surface.

6. A _____ does not have any edges or vertices, and has the same distance across any line through its center.

7. A _____ has one vertex, a circular base, and a curved surface.

8. A sphere has no _____ surfaces.

Name: _____ **Date:** _____

Find how many unit cubes are used to build each solid. *(Lesson 15.1)*

9.

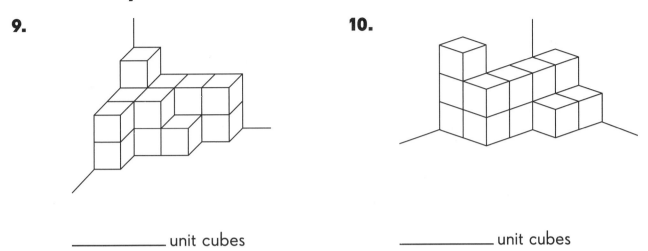

_____ unit cubes

10.

_____ unit cubes

Draw a cube with edges 2 times as long as the edges of this unit cube. *(Lesson 15.2)*

11.

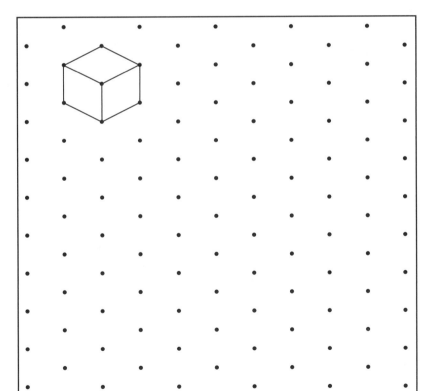

Complete the drawing of this rectangular prism. *(Lesson 15.2)*

12.

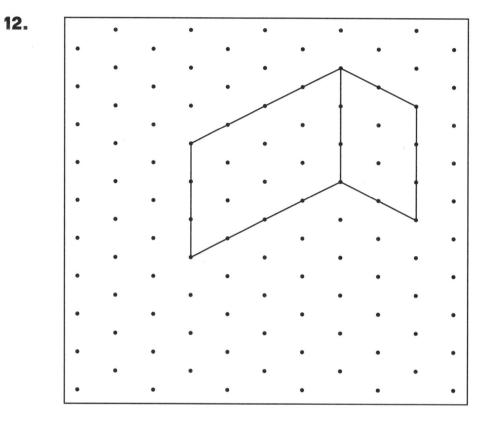

Find the surface area of each prism. *(Lesson 15.3)*

13.

 15 cm

18 cm   20 cm

14.

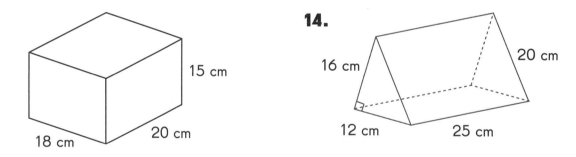

16 cm   20 cm

12 cm   25 cm

Name: _____ **Date:** _____

These solids are built using 1-inch cubes. Find and compare their volumes.
(Lesson 15.4)

15.

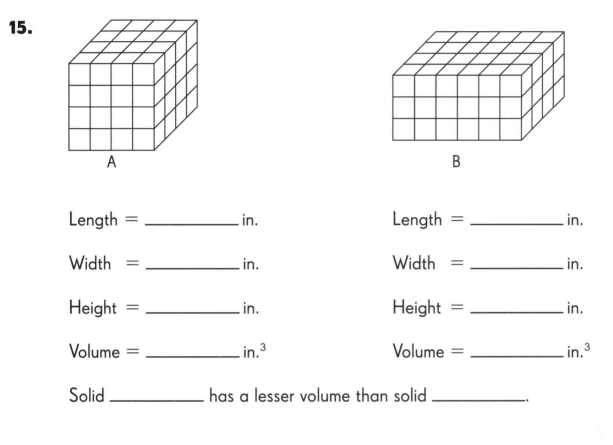

A   B

Length = _____ in.   Length = _____ in.

Width = _____ in.   Width = _____ in.

Height = _____ in.   Height = _____ in.

Volume = _____ in.^{3} Volume = _____ in.^{3}

Solid _____ has a lesser volume than solid _____.

Find the volume of each rectangular prism. *(Lesson 15.5)*

16.   **17.**

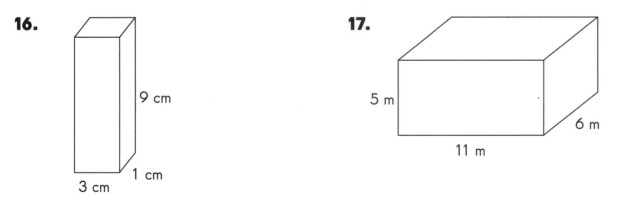

9 cm

1 cm

3 cm

5 m

11 m

6 m

Find the volume of water in each container in liters and milliliters.

(Lesson 15.5)

18.

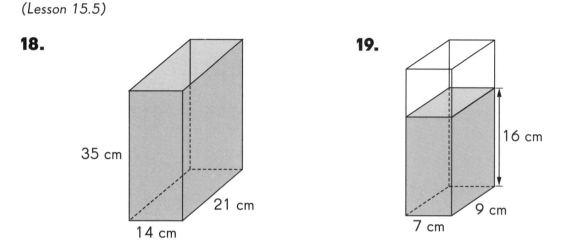

35 cm

14 cm

21 cm

19.

16 cm

7 cm

9 cm

Problem Solving

Solve. Show your work.

20. The length of a rectangular block is 20 inches. Its width is half its length. Its height is half its width. What is the surface area of the block?

Solve. Show your work.

21. A rectangular piece of poster board measures 70 centimeters by 50 centimeters. The net of a cube with 12-centimeter edges is cut from it. What is the area of the poster board left?

22. A rectangular prism is 15 inches long and 12 inches high. Its width is $\frac{3}{5}$ its length. Find its volume.

Solve. Show your work.

23. Three cubes with edges measuring 5 inches are stacked on top of one another. What is the total volume of the 3 cubes?

24. The rectangular container shown contains 2 liters of water. How much more water must be added to fill the container completely? Give your answer in liters.

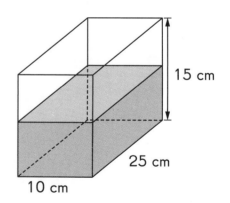

Name: _____ **Date:** _____

Solve. Show your work.

25. A container is 28 centimeters long, 14 centimeters wide, and 10 centimeters high. It is half-filled with juice. Kathy pours 500 milliliters of water into the container to make a juice drink. Find the volume of juice drink in the container now. Give your answer in liters and milliliters.

26. The fish tank shown is filled with 4 liters of water per minute from a faucet. How long does it take to fill the tank completely?

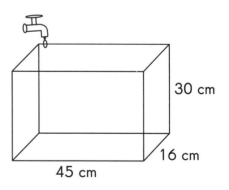

30 cm

16 cm

45 cm

Solve. Show your work.

27. A tank with a square base with edges measuring 20 centimeters and a height of 36 centimeters is $\frac{2}{3}$-filled with water. Each minute, 2 liters of water leak out of the tank through a crack in the bottom. How long does it take for all the water to leak out?

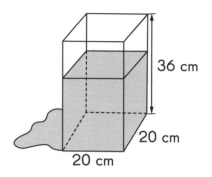

End-of-Year Review

Test Prep

Multiple Choice

Shade the circle next to the correct answer.

1. In 130.426, the digit 2 is in the _____ place. *(Lesson 8.1)*
   - (A) tens
   - (B) tenths
   - (C) hundredths
   - (D) thousandths

2. Use front-end estimation with adjustment to estimate 6,189 − 3,674. *(Lesson 1.4)*
   - (A) 1,000
   - (B) 2,000
   - (C) 3,000
   - (D) 4,000

3. Simplify $48 \div 8 + 13 \times 3$. *(Lesson 2.6)*
   - (A) 45
   - (B) 54
   - (C) 57
   - (D) 75

4. Express $10\frac{1}{4} - 4\frac{1}{2}$ as a decimal. *(Lesson 3.3)*
   - (A) 6.25
   - (B) 5.75
   - (C) 5.43
   - (D) 5.34

5. Express 9.062 as a mixed number in simplest form. *(Lesson 8.3)*
   - (A) $9\frac{62}{100}$
   - (B) $9\frac{31}{50}$
   - (C) $9\frac{62}{1000}$
   - (D) $9\frac{31}{500}$

6. What is the product of 96 and 13? *(Lesson 2.3)*
   - (A) 900
   - (B) 960
   - (C) 1,170
   - (D) 1,248

7. Divide 84 by 400. *(Lesson 9.4)*

(A) 0.21   (B) 0.84

(C) 2.1   (D) 8.4

8. Simplify $16p + 5 - 3p - 2$. *(Lesson 5.2)*

(A) $19p + 7$ (B) $19p - 3$

(C) $13p + 3$ (D) $13p - 3$

9. For what value of y will the inequality $4y - 8 > 10$ be true? *(Lesson 5.3)*

(A) 2   (B) 3

(C) 4   (D) 5

10. What percent of the figure is shaded? *(Lesson 10.1)*

(A) 25%   (B) 35%

(C) 40%   (D) 50%

11. The price of a cell phone is $500. Kathleen pays 8% sales tax on the price of the cell phone. How much sales tax does she pay? *(Lesson 10.4)*

(A) $400   (B) $50

(C) $40   (D) $8

12. $\overleftrightarrow{AB}$ and $\overleftrightarrow{CD}$ are lines. Find the measure of $\angle a$. *(Lesson 12.1)*

(A) 180°

(B) 105°

(C) 75°

(D) 57°

13. The sides of triangle *ABC* are in whole inches. *AB* = 5 inches and *BC* = 11 inches. Which of these is a possible length for $\overline{AC}$? *(Lesson 13.4)*

(A) 3 inches   (B) 6 inches

(C) 12 inches   (D) 16 inches

14. In the trapezoid *PQRS*, $\overline{PS} \parallel \overline{QR}$. Find the measure of $\angle SPR$. *(Lesson 13.5)*

(A) 98°

(B) 72°

(C) 52°

(D) 26°

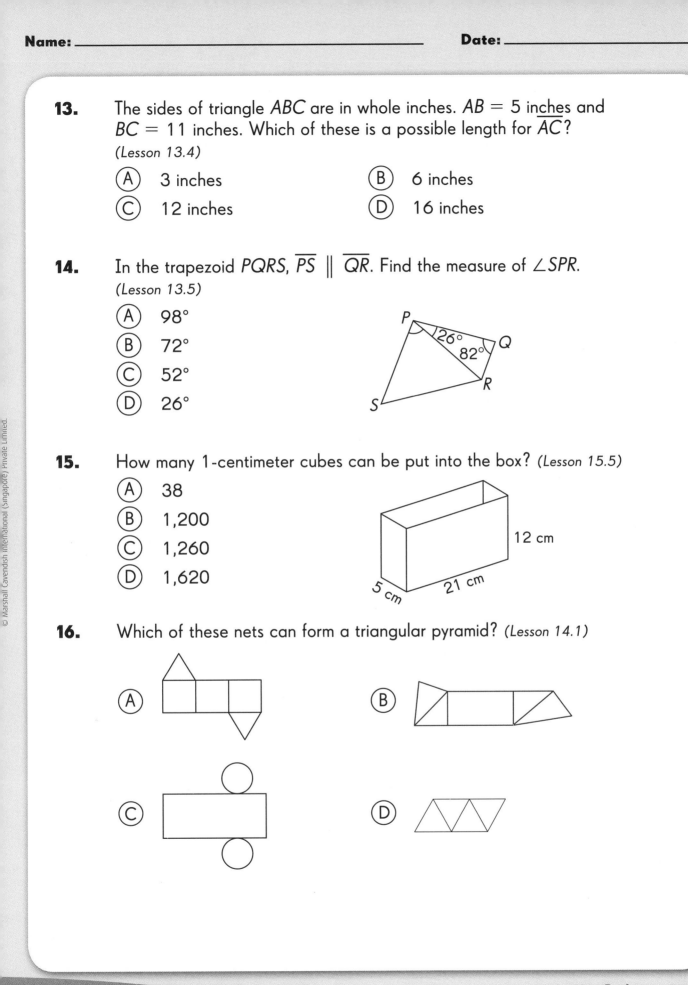

15. How many 1-centimeter cubes can be put into the box? *(Lesson 15.5)*

(A) 38

(B) 1,200

(C) 1,260

(D) 1,620

12 cm

5 cm   21 cm

16. Which of these nets can form a triangular pyramid? *(Lesson 14.1)*

(A)

(B)

(C)

(D)

Short Answer

Read the questions carefully. Write your answers in the spaces provided. Show your work.

17. The ratio of the volume of water in bucket A to the volume of water in bucket B is 3 : 5. The total volume of water in the two buckets is 56 liters. What is the volume of water in bucket B? *(Lesson 7.3)*

_____

18. Write 12 ones and 3 tenths 2 hundredths 5 thousandths in expanded form. *(Lesson 8.1)*

_____

19. What is the missing number in the equation? *(Lesson 9.4)*

$9.42 = 9{,}420 \div \boxed{}$ _____

20. Order the decimals from least to greatest. *(Lesson 8.2)*
11.05,   11.00,   11.10,   11.009

_____

21. $\frac{3}{8}$ of the regular price of a digital watch is $21. The price of the digital watch after discount is $21. Find the dollar amount of the discount.
(Lesson 10.4)

_____

Use the data in the bar graph to answer questions 22 and 23.

Favorite Sports of Students

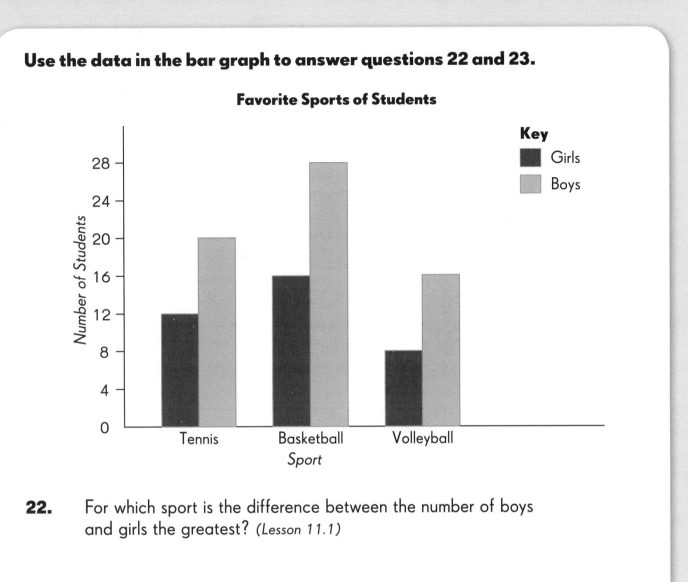

22. For which sport is the difference between the number of boys and girls the greatest? *(Lesson 11.1)*

_____

23. How many more boys than girls prefer tennis? *(Lesson 11.1)*

_____

Use the data in the graph to answer questions 24 and 25.

Conversion Between Gallons and Quarts

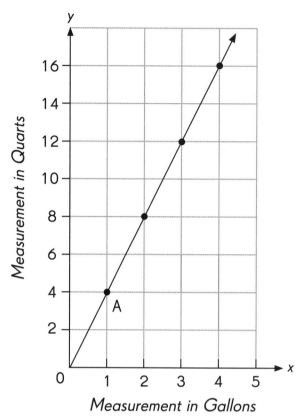

24. Mrs. Richards buys 8 quarts of milk in 4 days. How many gallons of milk does she buy? *(Lesson 11.2)*

_____

25. What is the equation of the graph? *(Lesson 11.2)*

_____

26. Mrs. Mani has 1 orange, 1 apple, 1 peach and 1 apricot. She has 3 different flavored yogurt bars. She packs one fruit and one yogurt bar into a lunch box. Find the number of combinations she can pack in one box. *(Lesson 11.3)*

_____

27. A box contains 6 red pens, 4 blue pens, 8 green pens, and some black pens. Leslie picks a pen and returns it to the box each time. The outcomes are recorded in the table.

Number of Times a Red Pen is Picked	Number of Times a Blue Pen is Picked	Number of Times a Green Pen is Picked	Number of Times a Black Pen is Picked
8	5	14	3

a. What is the experimental probability of drawing a green pen? *(Lesson 11.4)*

_____

b. If the theoretical probability of drawing a black pen is $\frac{1}{10}$, how many black pens are in the box? *(Lesson 11.4)*

_____

28. $\overleftrightarrow{AB}$, $\overleftrightarrow{CD}$ and $\overleftrightarrow{EF}$ are lines. Find the measures of $\angle x$ and $\angle y$.
(Lessons 12.1 and 12.3)

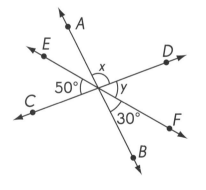

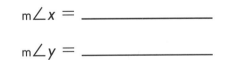

m$\angle x$ = _____

m$\angle y$ = _____

29. In triangle *DEF*, *DF* = *EF*. Find the measures of $\angle a$ and $\angle b$.
(Lessons 13.2 and 13.3)

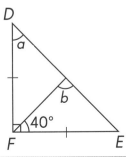

m$\angle a$ = _____

m$\angle b$ = _____

30. *ABCD* is a parallelogram and *ADE* is an equilateral triangle. Identify all the angles that have the same measure as ∠*f*. *(Lessons 13.3 and 13.5)*

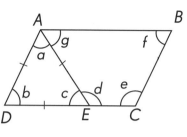

_____

31. Brian has $50. He buys 10 similar books and has *x* dollars left. What is the cost of each book? *(Lesson 5.4)*

_____

32. A solid figure has 2 flat surfaces, 1 curved surface, no edges and no vertices. Name this solid figure. *(Lesson 14.2)*

_____

33. How many unit cubes are used to build the solid? *(Lesson 15.1)*

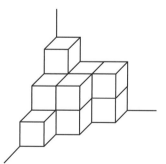

_____

34.   ABCD is a parallelogram. Find the measure of ∠DAC. (*Lesson 13.5*)

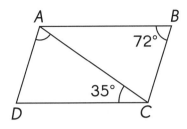

_____

35.   The net of a square prism is as given. Use the net to find the surface area of the prism. (*Lesson 15.3*)

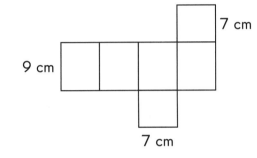

_____

36.   Express $3\frac{1}{5} + 2\frac{1}{20}$ as a decimal. (*Lesson 3.5*)

_____

37. $\overleftrightarrow{JL}$ is a line. Find the measure of ∠MKN. (*Lesson 12.1*)

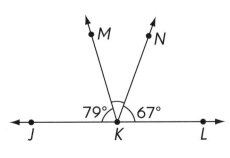

_____

Extended Response

Solve. Show your work.

38.   There are 450 seats in a theater. 48% of the seats are occupied. How many seats are not occupied?

39.   The area of a plot of land is 2,496 square meters. A small part of the land is fenced. The ratio of the total area of the plot of land to the area that is not fenced is 48 : 31. What is the area of the land that is not fenced?

40. Harry buys a sofa set that costs $2,000. He pays for it with 12 monthly installments. He also pays 5% interest. What is the total amount he has to pay?

41. Mrs. Jacobs buys 20 kilograms of rice at $0.84 per kilogram.
She buys 700 grams of shrimp at $1.02 per 100 grams.
How much does she spend in total?

42. A fish tank measures 40 centimeters by 25 centimeters by 24 centimeters. It is filled with water from a tap. The fish tank is $\frac{5}{8}$ full in 6 minutes. Find the volume of water that flows from the tap each minute.

43. Mrs. Jackson has $90. She spends $\frac{1}{4}$ of her money on food, $\frac{1}{2}$ of the remainder on clothes and saves the rest. How much does she save?

44. Team A has 42 members. Team B has 18 more members than team A. What percent of the members from team B must be transferred to team A so that team A has as many members as team B?

45. An equal amount of water is poured into two empty tanks, P and Q. Tank P is then $\frac{1}{2}$-filled. What fraction of tank Q is filled with water?

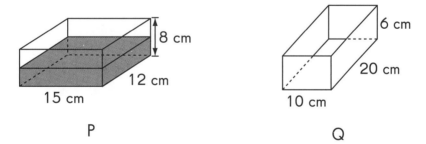

P

Q

46. There is some water in a tank. Water is then poured into the tank until the volume of water is 8 times as much as the initial volume of water in the tank. When another 16.75 liters of water is added, the total volume of water in the tank becomes 20.35 liters. How much water is in the tank at first? Give your answer in liters.